The Best of the World's Classics

VOL. VIII

CONTINENTAL EUROPE—II

TAINE

DANTE

GOETHE

CERVANTES

THE BEST
OF THE
WORLD'S
CLASSICS

RESTRICTED
TO PROSE

HENRY CABOT LODGE
EDITOR-IN-CHIEF

FRANCIS W. HALSEY
ASSOCIATE EDITOR

With an Introduction, Biographical and Explanatory
Notes, etc.

IN TEN VOLUMES

Vol. VIII
CONTINENTAL EUROPE—II

FUNK & WAGNALLS COMPANY
NEW YORK AND LONDON

CONTENTS

CONTENTS

CONTENTS

CONTENTS

CONTENTS

CONTENTS

FRANCE (Continued)

1805—1909

ALEXIS DE TOCQUEVILLE

Born in Paris in 1805, died in 1859; studied law, taking his degree in 1826; traveled in Italy and Sicily; in 1831 visited the United States under a commission to study the penitentiary system; returning published a book on the subject which was crowned by the French Academy; from private notes taken in America then wrote his masterpiece, "Democracy in America," which secured his election to the Academy in 1841; spent some years in public life and then retired in order to travel and write.

THE TYRANNY OF THE AMERICAN MAJORITY [1]

I HOLD it to be an impious and execrable maxim that, politically speaking, the people has a right to do whatever it pleases; and yet I have asserted that all authority originates in the will of the majority. Am I then in contradiction with myself?

A general law, which bears the name of justice, has been made and sanctioned not only by a majority of this or that people, but by a majority of mankind. The rights of every people are consequently confined within the limits of what is just. A nation may be considered in the light of a jury which is empowered to represent society at large and to apply the great and general law of justice. Ought such a jury, which represents society, to have more power than the society in which the law it applies originates?

[1] From Chapter XV of "Democracy in America." Translated by Henry Reeve.

3

When I refuse to obey an unjust law, I do not contest the right which the majority has of commanding, but I simply appeal from the sovereignty of the people to the sovereignty of mankind. It has been asserted that a people can never entirely outstep the boundaries of justice and of reason in those affairs which are more peculiarly its own; and that consequently, full power may fearlessly be given to the majority by which it is represented. But this language is that of a slave.

A majority, taken collectively, may be regarded as a being whose opinions, and most frequently whose interests are opposed to those of another being, which is styled a minority. If it be admitted that a man possessing absolute power may misuse that power by wronging his adversaries, why should a majority not be liable to the same reproach? Men are not apt to change their characters by agglomerating; nor does their patience in the presence of obstacles increase with the consciousness of their strength. And for these reasons I can never willingly invest any number of my fellow creatures with that unlimited authority which I should refuse to any one of them.

I do not think that it is possible to combine several principles in the same government so as at the same time to maintain freedom and really to oppose them to one another. The form of government which is usually termed mixt has always appeared to me to be a mere chimera. Accurately speaking, there is no such thing as a mixt government, with the meaning usually given to that word; because in all communities some one principle of action may be discovered which prepon-

4

derates over the others. England in the last century—which has been more especially cited as an example of this form of government—was in point of fact an essentially aristocratic state, altho it comprized very powerful elements of democracy; for the laws and customs of the country were such that the aristocracy could not but preponderate in the end, and subject the direction of public affairs to its own will. The error arose from too much attention being paid to the actual struggle that was going on between the nobles and the people, without considering the probable issue of the contest, which was really the important point. When a community actually has a mixt government—that is to say, when it is equally divided between two adverse principles—it must either pass through a revolution or fall into complete dissolution.

I am therefore of opinion that some one social power must always be made to predominate over the others; but I think that liberty is endangered when this power finds no obstacle which can retard its course, and force it to moderate its own vehemence.

Unlimited power is in itself a bad and dangerous thing. Human beings are not competent to exercise it with discretion. God only can be omnipotent, because His wisdom and His justice are always equal to His power. But no power on earth is so worthy of honor for itself that I would consent to admit its uncontrolled and all-predominant authority. When I see that the right and the means of absolute command or of reverential obedience to the right which it represents are conferred on a people or upon a king, upon an aristocracy or a democracy, a monarchy or a republic, I recognize the germ of tyranny; and I journey onward to a land of more hopeful institutions.

In my opinion, the main evil of the present democratic institutions of the United States does not arise, as is often asserted in Europe, from their weakness, but from their irresistible strength. I am not so much alarmed at the excessive liberty which reigns in that country as at the very inadequate securities which exist against tyranny.

When an individual or a party is wronged in the United States, to whom can he apply for redress? If to public opinion, public opinion constitutes the majority; if to the legislature, it represents the majority, and implicitly obeys its instructions; if to the executive power, it is appointed by the majority, and is a passive tool in its hands. The public troops consist of the majority under arms; the jury is the majority invested with the right of hearing judicial cases; and in certain cases, even the judges are elected by the majority. However iniquitous or absurd the evil of which you complain may be, you must submit to it as well as you can.

If, on the other hand, a legislative power could be so constituted as to represent the majority without necessarily being the slave of its passions, an executive so as to retain a certain degree of uncontrolled authority, and a judiciary so as to remain independent of the other two powers, a government would be formed which would still be democratic, without incurring any risk of tyranny.

I do not say that there is a frequent use of tyranny in America at the present day; but I maintain that no sure barrier is established against it, and that the causes which mitigate the government are to be found in the circumstances and the manners of the country more than in its laws.

ALFRED DE MUSSET

Born in 1810, died in 1857; educated at the College of
Henry II in Paris; published "Tales of Spain and Italy,"
a volume of verse, in 1829; followed by other collections of
verse in 1831 and 1832; went to Italy in 1833 with George
Sand, with whom he quarreled in Venice and returned to
France; published "Confessions of a Child of the Century"
in 1836; wrote stories and plays as well as poems; elected
to the Academy in 1852.

TITIAN'S SON AFTER A NIGHT AT PLAY [1]

IN the month of February of the year 1580 a
young man was crossing the Piazzeta at Venice
at early dawn. His clothes were in disorder, his
cap, from which hung a beautiful scarlet feather,
was pulled down over his ears. He was walking
with long strides toward the banks of the Schia-
voni, and his sword and cloak were dragging
behind him, while with a somewhat disdainful
foot he picked his way among the fishermen lying

[1] From De Musset's story, "Titian's Son." Translated for
this collection by Eric Arthur Bell. Titian's son, who was
named Pomponio, had been destined for the Church, but
proving wasteful and dissipated, his father caused the ben-
efice intended for him to be transferred to a nephew.
Through the death of Titian's other son Orazio, an artist of
repute, who died soon after Titian and during the same
plague, Pomponio inherited the handsome fortune his father
had left and completely squandered it.

asleep on the ground. Having arrived at the bridge of Paille, he stopt and looked around him. The moon was setting behind the Giudecca and the dawn was gilding the Ducal Palace. From time to time thick smoke or a brilliant light could be seen from some neighboring palace. Planks, stones, enormous blocks of marble, and debris of every kind obstructed the Canal of the Prisons. A recent fire had just destroyed the home of a patrician which lined its banks. A volley of sparks shot up from time to time, and by this sinister light an armed soldier could be seen keeping watch in the midst of the ruins.

Our young man, however, did not seem to be imprest either with this spectacle of destruction or with the beauty of the sky, tinged with the rosy colors of the dawning day. He looked for some time at the horizon, as if to ease his tired eyes; but the brightness of the dawn seemed to produce in him a disagreeable effect, for he wrapt himself in his cloak and pursued his way at a run. He soon stopt again at the door of a palace, where he knocked. A valet, holding a torch in his hand, admitted him immediately. As he entered he turned round, and casting one more glance at the sky, exclaimed, "By Bacchus! my carnival has cost me dear."

This young man was called Pomponio Filippo Vecellio. He was the second son of Titian, a youth full of spirit and imagination who had aroused in his father the most lofty expectations, but whose passion for cards kept him in continual dissipation. It was only four years before that the great painter and his eldest son, Orazio, had died almost at the same time, and young

Pippo in those four years had already dissipated the best part of the immense fortune which the double heritage had given him. Instead of cultivating the talents which he possest by nature and sustaining the glory of his name, he passed his days in sleeping and his nights in playing at the house of a certain Countess Orsini, or at least so-called countess, who made a profession of ruining the gilded youth of Venice. Every night there assembled at her house a large company composed of nobles and courtezans; there one supped and played, and as one did not pay for one's supper, it goes without saying that the dice helped to indemnify the mistress of the house. Meanwhile, the sequins and the Cyprian wine began to flow freely, loving glances were exchanged, and the victims, drunk with love and wine, lost their money and their reason.

It is from this dangerous resort that we have seen the hero of this story emerge. He had met with more than one loss during the night. Besides having emptied his pockets at cards; the only picture he had ever finished, one that the connoisseurs had pronounced excellent, had just been destroyed in a fire in the Dolfino palace. It was an historical subject, treated with a spirit and a sureness of touch almost worthy of Titian himself. Sold to a rich Senator, this canvas had met with the same fate as a great number of other previous works of art; the carelessness of a valet had turned it to ashes. But this Pippo counted the least of his misfortunes; he was only thinking of the unlucky star that had lately been following him with unusual insistence and of the throws of dice it had made him lose.

On entering his house, he began by taking off the coverlet which lay on his table and counting the money left in his drawer; then, as he was of a nature naturally gay and optimistic, after he had undrest he sat at the window in his night robe. Seeing that it was almost daylight, he began to ponder whether he would close the shutters and get into bed, or get up like everybody else. It was a long time since he had seen the sun in the east, and he found the sky more beautiful than ever. Before deciding whether to wake up or go to sleep, he took his chocolate on the balcony, in an effort to fight off his drowsiness. The moment his eyes closed, he would see a table, many trembling hands and pale faces, and would hear again the sound of the cornets. "What fatal luck," he murmured. "Is it possible that one can lose with fifteen?" And he saw his habitual opponent, old Vespiano Memmo, throwing eighteen and taking up the money piled on the table.

He promptly opened his eyelids to get rid of the bad dream, and looked at the young girls passing on the quay. He seemed to see in the distance a masked woman; and was astonished, altho it was the time of carnival, for poor people do not go masked, and it was strange that at such an hour a Venetian lady should be out alone on foot. He perceived, however, that what he had taken for a mask was the face of a negress. On getting a nearer look at her, he saw she was not badly formed. She walked very quickly, and a puff of wind which forced her checkered skirt close to her limbs, showed her to have a graceful figure. Pippo leaned over the balcony and saw not without surprize that the negress knocked at his door.

The porter failed to open it.

"What do you want?" cried the young man. "Is it with me that your business lies, brunette? My name is Vecellio, and if they are going to keep you waiting, I will come and let you in myself."

The negress lifted her head.

"Your name is Pomponio Vecellio?"

"Yes, or Pippo, whichever you like."

"You are the son of Titian?"

"At your service. What can I do to please you?"

Having cast on Pippo a rapid and curious glance, the negress took a few steps backward, and skilfully threw up into the balcony a little box rolled in paper, and then promptly fled, turning round from time to time. Pippo picked up the box, opened it, and found a pretty purse wrapt in cotton. He rightly suspected that he might find under the cotton a note that would explain this adventure. The note was found indeed, but it was as mysterious as the rest, for it contained only these words: "Do not spend too readily what I enclose herein; when you leave home, charge me with one piece of gold. It is enough for one day; and if in the evening you have any of it left, however little, it may be you will find some poor person who will thank you for it."

The young man examined the box in a hundred different ways, scrutinized the purse, looked once more on to the quay, and at length realized that he had learned all he could. "Of a truth," thought he, "this is a strange present, but it comes at a cruelly awkward moment. The advice they give me is good, but it is too late to tell people to swim when they are already at the bottom of the Adriatic. Who the devil could have sent me this?"

THEOPHILE GAUTIER

Born in 1811, died in 1872; studied painting in Paris, but soon joined the romantic literary movement; his first book, "Poèsies," published in 1830; an art and dramatic critic 1837-45; traveled in Spain, Holland, Italy, Greece and Russia in 1840-58, publishing books describing those countries and novels with them for scenes; many other novels followed, with occasional collections of verse and criticism.

PHARAOH'S ENTRY INTO THEBES [1]

AT length their chariot reached the maneuvering-ground, an immense enclosure, carefully leveled, used for splendid military displays. Terraces, one above the other, which must have employed for years the thirty nations led away into slavery, formed a frame *en relief* for the gigantic parallelogram; sloping walls built of crude bricks lined these terraces; their tops were covered, several rows deep, by hundreds of thousands of Egyptians, whose white or brightly colored costumes blazed in the sun with that perpetually restless movement which characterizes a multitude, even when it appears motionless; behind this line of spectators the cars, chariots, and litters, with their drivers, grooms, and slaves, looked like the encampment of an emigrating nation, such was their immense number; for Thebes, the marvel of the ancient world, counted more inhabitants than did some kingdoms.

[1] From the "Romance of a Mummy." Translated by M. Young, as authorized by Gautier.

14

The fine, even sand of the vast arena, bordered with a million heads, gleamed like mica dust beneath the light, falling from a sky as blue as the enamel on the statuettes of Osiris. On the south side of the field the terraces were broken, making way for a road which stretched toward Upper Ethiopia, the whole length of the Libyan chain. In the corresponding corner, the opening in the massive brick walls prolonged the roads to the Rhamses-Maïamoun palace. . . .

A frightful uproar, rumbling, deep, and mighty as that of an approaching sea, arose in the distance, and drowned the thousand murmurs of the crowd, like the roar of the lion which hushes the barking of the jackals. Soon the noise of instruments of music could be distinguished amidst this terrestrial thunder, produced by the chariot wheels and the rhythmic pace of the foot-soldiers. A sort of reddening cloud, like that raised by the desert blasts, filled the sky in that direction, yet the wind had gone down; there was not a breath of air, and the smallest branches of the palm-trees hung motionless, as if they had been carved on a granite capital; not a hair moved on the women's moist foreheads, and the fluted streamers of their head-dresses hung loosely down their backs. This powdery fog was caused by the marching army, and hung over it like a fallow cloud.

The tumult increased; the whirlwinds of dust opened, and the first files of musicians entered the immense arena, to the great satisfaction of the multitude, who in spite of its respect for his Majesty were beginning to tire of waiting beneath a sun which would have melted any other skulls

15

than those of the Egyptians. The advance guard
of musicians halted for several instants; colleges
of priests, deputations of the principal inhabitants of Thebes, crossed the maneuvering-ground
to meet the Pharaoh, and arranged themselves in
a row in postures of the most profound respect,
in such manner as to give free passage to the
procession. The band, which alone was a small
army, consisted of drums, tabors, trumpets, and
sistras.

The first squad passed, blowing a deafening
blast upon their short clarions of polished brass
which shone like gold. Each of these trumpeters
carried a second horn under his arm, as if the
instrument might grow weary sooner than the
man. The costume of these men consisted of a
short tunic, fastened by a sash with ends falling
in front; a small band, in which were stuck two
ostrich-feathers hanging over on either side,
bound their thick hair. These plumes, so worn,
recalled to mind the antennæ of scarabæi, and
gave the wearers an odd look of being insects.

The drummers, clothed in a simple gathered
skirt, and naked to the waist, beat the onagra-
skin heads of their rounded drums with sycamore-
wood drumsticks, their instruments suspended by
leather shoulder-belts, and observed the time
which a drum-major marked for them by re-
peatedly turning toward them and clapping his
hands. After the drummers came the sistra-
players, who shook their instruments by a quick,
abrupt motion, and made at measured intervals
the metal links ring on the four bronze bars.
The tabor-players carried their oblong instruments crosswise, held up by a scarf passed around

the neck, and struck the lightly stretched parchment with both hands.

Each company of musicians numbered at least two hundred men; but the hurricane of noise produced by trumpets, drums, tabors, and sistras, and which would have drawn blood from the ears inside a palace, was none too loud or too unbearable beneath the vast cupola of heaven, in the midst of this immense open space, amongst this buzzing crowd, at the head of this army which would baffle nomenclators, and which was now advancing with a roar as of great waters.

After the musicians came the barbarian captives, strangely formed, with brutish faces, black skins, woolly hair, resembling apes as much as men, and drest in the costume of their country, a short skirt above the hips, held by a single brace, embroidered in different colors. An ingenious and whimsical cruelty had suggested the way in which the prisoners were chained. Some were bound with their elbows drawn behind their backs; others with their hands lifted above their heads, in a still more painful position; one had his wrists fastened in wooden cangs (instruments of torture, still used in China); another was half-strangled in a sort of pillory; or a chain of them were linked together by the same rope, each victim having a knot round his neck. It seemed as if those who had bound these unfortunates had found a pleasure in forcing them into unnatural positions; and they advanced before their conqueror with awkward and tottering gait, rolling their large eyes and contorted with pain. Guards walked beside them, regulating their step by beating them with staves. . . . .

A wide gorget with seven rows of enamels, precious stones, and golden beads fell over the Pharaoh's chest and gleamed brightly in the sunlight. His upper garment was a sort of loose shirt, with pink and black squares; the ends, lengthening into narrow slips, were wound several times about his bust and bound it closely; the sleeves, cut short near the shoulder, and bordered with intersecting lines of gold, red, and blue, exposed his round, strong arms, the left furnished with a large metal wristband, meant to lessen the vibration of the string when he discharged an arrow from his triangular bow; and the right, ornamented by a bracelet in the form of a serpent in several coils, held a long gold scepter with a lotus bud at the end. The rest of his body was wrapt in drapery of the finest linen, minutely plaited, bound about the waist by a belt inlaid with small enamel and gold plates. Between the band and the belt his torso appeared, shining and polished like pink granite shaped by a cunning workman. Sandals with returned toes, like skates, shod his long narrow feet, placed together like those of the gods on the temple walls.

His smooth beardless face, with large clearly cut features, which it seemed beyond any human power to disturb, and which the blood of common life did not color, with its death-like pallor, sealed lips, enormous eyes enlarged with black lines, the lids no more lowered than those of the sacred hawk, inspired by its very immobility a feeling of respectful fear. One might have thought that these fixt eyes were searching for eternity and the Infinite; they never seemed to rest on surrounding objects. The satiety of pleasures, the surfeit of wishes satisfied as soon as exprest, the isolation of a demigod who has no equal among mortals, the disgust for perpetual adoration, and as it were weariness of continual triumph, had forever frozen this face, implacably gentle and of granite serenity. Osiris judging the souls could not have had a more majestic and calm expression. A large tame lion, lying by his side, stretched out its enormous paws like a sphinx on its pedestal, and blinked its yellow eyes.

A rope, attached to the litter, bound the war chariots of the vanquished chiefs to the Pharaoh. He dragged them behind him like animals in leash. These men, with fierce despairing faces, their elbows drawn together by a strap and forming an ungraceful angle, tottered awkwardly at every motion of the chariots, driven by Egyptians.

Next came the chariots of the young princes royal, drawn by thoroughbred horses, elegantly and nobly formed, with slender legs, sinewy houghs, their manes cut short like a brush, harnessed by twos, tossing their red-plumed heads, with metal-bossed headstalls and frontlets. A curved pole, upheld on their withers, covered with scarlet panels, two collars surmounted by balls of polished brass, bound together by a light yoke bent like a bow with upturned ends; a bellyband and breastband elaborately stitched and embroidered, and rich housings with red or blue stripes and fringed with tassels, completed this strong, graceful, and light harness. . . .

In the wake of the princes followed the chariots, the Egyptian cavalry, twenty thousand in number, each drawn by two horses and holding three men. They advanced ten in a line, the axletrees perilously near together, but never coming in contact with each other, so great was the address of the drivers.

The stamping of the horses, held in with difficulty, the thundering of the bronze-covered wheels, the metallic clash of weapons, gave to this line something formidable and imposing enough to raise terror in the most intrepid bosoms. The helmets, plumes, and breastplates dotted with red, green, and yellow, the gilded bows and brass swords, glittered and blazed terribly in the light of the sun, open in the sky, above the Libyan chain, like a great Osirian eye; and it was felt that the onslaught of such an army must sweep away the nations like a whirlwind which drives a light straw before it.

Beneath these innumerable wheels the earth resounded and trembled, as if it had been moved by some convulsion of nature.

To the chariots succeeded the battalions of infantry, marching in order, their shields on the left arm; in the right hand the lance, curved club, bow, sling, or ax, according as they were armed; the heads of these soldiers were covered with helmets, adorned with two horsehair tails, their bodies girded with a cuirass belt of crocodileskin. Their impassible look, the perfect regularity of their movements, their reddish copper complexions, deepened by a recent expedition to the burning regions of Upper Ethiopia, their clothing powdered with the desert sand, they awoke admiration by their discipline and courage. With soldiers like those Egypt could conquer the world. After them came the allied troops, recognizable from the outlandish form of their headpieces, which looked like truncated miters, or were surmounted by crescents spitted on sharp points. Their wide-bladed swords and jagged axes must have produced wounds which could not be healed.

Slaves carried on their shoulders or on barrows the spoils enumerated by the herald, and wild-beast tamers dragged behind them leashed panthers, cheetahs, crouching down as if trying to hide themselves, ostriches fluttering their wings, giraffes which overtopped the crowd by the entire length of their necks, and even brown bears—taken, they said, in the Mountains of the Moon.

The procession was still passing, long after the King had entered his palace.

GUSTAVE FLAUBERT

Born in 1821, died in 1880; traveled in the East; published in 1857 his best-known work, "Madame Bovary," which led to litigation as to the morality of the story; ultimately acquitted; published "Salâmmbo" in 1858; author of other novels and plays.

YONGEVILLE AND ITS PEOPLE[1]

YONVILLE-L'ABBAYE — so called from an old Capuchin abbey of which not even the ruins remain—is a market-town twenty-four miles from Rouen, between the Abbeville and Beauvais roads, at the foot of a valley watered by the Rieule, a little river that runs into the Andelle after turning three water-mills near its mouth, where there are a few trout that the lads amuse themselves by fishing for on Sundays.

We leave the highroad at a Boissière and keep straight on to the top of Leux hill, whence the valley is seen. The river that runs through it makes of it, as it were, two regions with distinct physiognomies—all on the left is pasture land, all on the right arable. The meadow stretches under a bulge of low hills to join at the back with the pasture land of the Bray country, while on the eastern side the plain, gently rising, broadens out, showing as far as eye can follow its blonde corn-fields. The water, flowing by the

[1] From Part II of "Madame Bovary." Translated by Eleanor Marx-Aveling. Copyright, 1901, by George Munro's Sons.

grass, divides with a white line the color of the roads and of the plains, and the country is like a great unfolded mantle with a green velvet cape bordered with a fringe of silver.

Before us, on the verge of the horizon, lie the oaks of the forest of Argueil, with the steeps of St. Jean hills scarred from top to bottom with red irregular lines; they are rain-tracks, and these brick tones, standing out in narrow streaks against the gray color of the mountain, are due to the quantity of iron springs that flow beyond in the neighboring country.

Here we are on the confines of Normandy, Picardy, and the Ile-de-France, a bastard land, whose language is without accent as its landscape is without character. It is there that they make the worst Neuchâtel cheeses of all the *arrondissement;* and, on the other hand, farming is costly because so much manure is needed to enrich this friable soil, full of sand and flints.

Up to 1835 there was no practicable road for getting to Yonville; but about this time a cross-road was made which joins that of Abbeville to that of Amiens, and is occasionally used by the Rouen wagoners on their way to Flanders. Yonville-l'Abbaye has remained stationary in spite of its ''new outlet.'' Instead of improving the soil, they persist in keeping up the pasture-lands, however depreciated they may be in value, and the lazy borough, growing away from the plain, has naturally spread riverward. It is seen from afar sprawling along the banks like a cow-herd taking a siesta by the water-side.

At the foot of the hill beyond the bridge begins a roadway, planted with young aspens, that leads in a straight line to the first houses in the place. These, fenced in by hedges, are in the middle of courtyards full of straggling buildings, wine-presses, cart-sheds, and distilleries scattered under thick trees, with ladders, poles, or scythes hung on to the branches. The thatched roofs, like fur caps drawn over eyes, reach down over about a third of the low windows, whose coarse convex glasses have knots in the middle like the bottoms of bottles. Against the plaster wall, diagonally crossed by black joists, a meager pear-tree sometimes leans, and the ground floors have at their door a small swing-gate, to keep out the chicks that come pilfering crumbs of bread steeped in cider on the threshold. But the court-yards grow narrower, the houses closer together, and the fences disappear; a bundle of ferns swings under a window from the end of a broom-stick; there is a blacksmith's forge and then a wheelwright's, with two or three new carts out-side that partly block up the way. Then across an open space appears a white house beyond a grass mound ornamented by a cupid, his finger on his lips; two brass vases are at each end of a flight of steps; scutcheons blaze upon the door. It is the notary's house, and the finest in the place.

The church is on the other side of the street, twenty paces farther down, at the entrance of the square. The little cemetery that surrounds it, closed in by a wall breast-high, is so full of graves that the old stones, level with the ground, form a continuous pavement, on which the grass of itself has marked out regular green squares. The church was rebuilt during the last years of the reign of Charles X. The wooden roof is beginning to rot from the top, and here and there has black hollows in its blue color. Over the door, where the organ should be, is a loft for the men, with a spiral staircase that reverberates under their wooden shoes.

The daylight coming through the plain glass windows falls obliquely upon the pews ranged along the walls, which are adorned here and there with a straw mat bearing beneath it the words in large letters, "Mr. So-and-So's pew." Farther on, at the spot where the building narrows, the confessional forms a pendant to a statuette of the Virgin, clothed in a satin robe, coifed with a tulle veil sprinkled with silver stars, and with red cheeks, like an idol of the Sandwich Islands, and, finally, a copy of the "Holy Family, presented by the Minister of the Interior," overlooking the high altar, between four candlesticks, closes in the perspective. The choir stalls, of deal wood, have been left unpainted.

The market—that is to say, a tiled roof supported by some twenty posts—occupies of itself about half the public square of Yonville. The town-hall, constructed "from the designs of a Paris architect," is a sort of Greek temple that forms the corner next to the chemist's shop. On the ground floor are three Ionic columns, and on the first floor is a semicircular gallery, while the dome that crowns it is occupied by a Gallic cock, resting one foot upon the "Charte" and holding in the other the scales of Justice.

But that which most attracts the eye is, opposite the Lion d'Or inn, the chemist's shop of Monsieur Homais. In the evening especially its argand lamp is lighted up, and the red and green jars that embellish his shop-front throw far across the street their two streams of color; then across them, as if in Bengal lights, is seen the shadow of the chemist leaning over his desk. His house from top to bottom is placarded with inscriptions written in large hand, round hand, printed hand: "Vichy, Seltzer, Barège waters, blood purifiers, Raspail patent medicine, Arabian racahout, Darcet lozenges, Regnault paste, trusses, baths, hygienic chocolate," etc. And the signboard, which takes up all the breadth of the shop, bears, in gold letters, "Homais, Chemist." Then, at the back of the shop, behind the great scales fixt to the counter, the word "Laboratory" appears on a scroll above a glass door, which about half-way up once more repeats "Homais" in gold letters on a black ground.

Beyond this there is nothing to see at Yonville. The street—the only one—a gunshot in length, and flanked by a few shops on each side, stops short at the turn of the highroad. If it is left to the right hand and the foot of the St. Jean hills followed, the cemetery is soon reached.

At the time of the cholera, in order to enlarge this, a piece of wall was pulled down, and three acres of land by its side purchased; but all the new portion is almost tenantless; the tombs, as heretofore, continue to crowd together toward the gate. The keeper, who is at once grave-digger and church-beadle—thus making a double profit out of the parish corpses—has taken advantage of the unused plot of ground to plant potatoes there. From year to year, however, his small field grows smaller, and when there is an epidemic, he does not know whether to rejoice at the deaths or regret the burials.

"You live on the dead, Lestiboudois!" the curé at last said to him one day. This grim remark made him reflect; it checked him for some time; but to this day he carries on the cultivation of his little tubers, and even maintains stoutly that they grow naturally.

Since the events about to be narrated, nothing in fact has changed at Yonville. The tin tricolor flag swings at the top of the church-steeple; the two chintz streamers still flutter in the wind from the linen-draper's; the chemist's fetuses, like lumps of white amadou, rot more and more in their turbid alcohol, and above the big door of the inn the old golden lion, faded by rain, still shows passers-by its poodle mane.

On the evening when the Bovarys were to arrive at Yonville, Widow Lefrançois, the landlady of this inn, was so very busy that she sweated great drops as she moved her saucepans. Tomorrow was market-day. The meat had to be cut beforehand, the fowls drawn, the soup and coffee made. Moreover, she had the boarders' meal to see to, and that of the doctor, his wife, and their servant; the billiard-room was echoing with bursts of laughter; three millers in the small parlor were calling for brandy; the wood was blazing, the brazen pan was hissing, and on the long kitchen-table, amid the quarters of raw mutton, rose piles of plates that rattled with the shaking of the block on which spinach was being chopped. From the poultry-yard was heard the screaming of the fowls whom the servant was chasing in order to wring their necks.

A man slightly marked with smallpox, in green leather slippers, and wearing a velvet cap with a gold tassel was warming his back at the chimney. His face exprest nothing but self-satisfaction, and he appeared to take life as calmly as the goldfinch suspended over his head in its wicker cage—this was the chemist.

"Artémise!" shouted the landlady, "chop some wood, fill the water-bottles, bring some brandy, look sharp! If only I knew what dessert to offer the guests you are expecting! Good heavens! Those furniture-movers are beginning their racket in the billiard-room again; and their van has been left before the front door! The Hirondelle might run into it when it draws up. Call Polyte and tell him to put it up. Only to think, Monsieur Homais, that since morning they have had about fifteen games and drunk eight jars of cider! Why, they'll tear my cloth for me," she went on, looking at them from a distance, her strainer in her hand.

"That wouldn't be much of a loss," replied Monsieur Homais. "You would buy another."

"Another billiard-table," exclaimed the widow.

"Since that one is coming to pieces, Madame Lefrançois. I tell you again you are doing yourself harm, much harm! And besides, players now want narrow pockets and heavy cues. Hazards aren't played now; everything is changed! One must keep pace with the times! Just look at Tellier!"

The hostess reddened with vexation. The chemist went on:

"You may say what you like; his table is better than yours; and if one were to think, for example, of getting up a patriotic pool for Poland or the sufferers from the Lyons floods—''

''It isn't beggars like him that'll frighten us,'' interrupted the landlady, shrugging her fat shoulders. ''Come, come, Monsieur Homais; as long as the Lion d'Or exists people will come to it. We've feathered our nest; while one of these days you'll find the Café Français closed with a big placard on the shutters. Change my billiard-table!'' she went on, speaking to herself, ''the table that comes in so handy for folding the washing, and on which, in the hunting season, I have slept six visitors! But that dawdler Hivert doesn't come!''

''Are you waiting for him for your gentlemen's dinner?''

''Wait for him! And what about Monsieur Binet? As the clock strikes six you'll see him come in, for he hasn't his equal under the sun for punctuality. He must always have his seat in the small parlor. He'd rather die than dine anywhere else. And so squeamish as he is, and so particular about the cider! Not like Monsieur Léon; he sometimes comes at seven, or even half-past, and he doesn't so much as look at what he eats. Such a nice young man! Never speaks a rough word!''

''Well, you see, there's a great difference between an educated man and an old carabineer who is now a tax-collector.''

JOSEPH ERNEST RENAN

Born in 1823, died in 1892; a teacher and a student of comparative philology; began to publish in 1850 books which attracted attention for their excellence of style; traveled in the East in 1861; called to the chair of history in the College of France, but forced to resign because he denied the divinity of Christ; published his "Life of Jesus" in 1863, "The Apostles," in 1866, "St. Paul" in 1867, "L'Anté-Christ" in 1873, "The Christian Church" in 1879, "Marcus Aurelius" in 1880, and "History of the People of Israel" in 1887-94; elected to the French Academy in 1878.

AN EMPIRE IN ROBUST YOUTH [1]

THE political condition of the world was most melancholy. All power was concentrated at Rome and in the legions. The most shameful and degrading scenes were daily enacted. The Roman aristocracy, which had conquered the world, and which alone of all the people had any voice in public business under the Cæsars, had abandoned itself to a saturnalia of the most outrageous wickedness the human race ever witnessed. Cæsar and Augustus, in establishing the imperial power, saw perfectly the necessities of the age. The world was so low in its political relations that no other form of government was possible. Now that Rome had conquered numberless prov-

[1] From the "History of the Origins of Christianity," the same being a series of which the first book was "The Life of Jesus." This passage is from the second volume which is entitled "The Apostles." From an anonymous translation, published in 1866 by Carleton, of New York.

inces, the ancient constitution, which was based upon the existence of a privileged patrician class, a kind of obstinate and malevolent Tories, could not continue.

But Augustus had signally neglected every suggestion of true policy by leaving the future to chance. Destitute of any canon of hereditary succession, of any settled rules concerning adoption, and of any law regulating election, Cæsarism was like an enormous load on the deck of a vessel without ballast. The most terrible shocks were inevitable. Three times in a century, under Caligula, Nero, and Domitian, the greatest power that was ever united in one person fell into the hands of most extravagant and execrable men. Horrors were enacted which have hardly been surpassed by the monsters of the Mongol dynasties. In that fatal list of monarchs one is reduced to apologizing for a Tiberius, who only attained thorough detestableness toward the close of his life; and for a Claudius, who was only eccentric, blundering, and badly advised.

Rome became a school of vice and cruelty. It should be added that the vice came, in a great degree, from the East, from those parasites of low rank and those infamous men whom Egypt and Syria sent to Rome, and who, profiting by the oppression of the true Romans, succeeded in attaining great influence over the wretches who governed. The most disgusting ignominies of the empire, such as the apotheosis of the emperors and their deification during life, came from the East, and particularly from Egypt, which was at that period one of the most corrupt countries on the face of the earth.

However, the veritable Roman nature still survived, and nobility of soul was far from extinct. The lofty traditions of pride and virtue, which were preserved in a few families, attained the imperial throne with Nerva, and gave its splendor to the age of the Antonines, of which Tacitus is the elegant historian. An age in which such true and noble natures as those of Quintilian, Tacitus, and Pliny the Younger were produced need not be wholly despaired of. The corruption of the surface did not extend to the great mass of seriousness and honor which existed in the better Roman society, and many examples are yet preserved of devotion to order, duty, peace, and solid integrity. There were in the noble houses admirable wives and sisters. Was there ever a more touching fate than that of the young and chaste Octavia, the daughter of Claudius, and wife of Nero, remaining pure in the midst of infamy, and slain at twenty-two years of age, without having known a single joy? The epithets "castissimo," "univiro,"[2] are not at all rare in the inscriptions. Some wives accompanied their husbands into exile, and others shared their noble deaths. The ancient Roman simplicity was not lost. The children were soberly and carefully brought up. The most noble ladies worked with their own hands at woolen fabrics, and the excesses of the toilet were almost unknown in the higher families.

The excellent statesmen who, so to speak, sprang from the earth under Trajan, were not improvised. They had served in preceding reigns;

[2] These epitaphs mean respectively "the most chaste" and "the wife of one husband."

but they had enjoyed but little influence, and had been cast into the shade by the freedmen and favorite slaves of the Emperor. Thus we find men of the first ability occupying high posts under Nero. The framework was good. The accession of bad emperors, disastrous as it was, could not change at once the general tendency of affairs, and the principles of the government. The empire, far from being in its decay, was in the full strength of vigorous youth. Decay will come, but two centuries later; and, strange to say, under much more worthy monarchs. In its political phase the situation was analogous to that of France, which, deprived by the revolution of any established rule for the succession, has yet passed through so many perilous changes without greatly injuring its internal organization or its national strength. In its moral aspect, the period under consideration may be compared to the eighteenth century, an epoch entirely corrupt, if we form our judgment from the memoirs, manuscripts, literature, and anecdotes of the time, but in which, nevertheless, some families maintained the greatest austerity of morals.

Philosophy joined hands with the better families of Rome, and resisted nobly. The stoic school produced the lofty characters of Cremutius Cordus, Thraseas, Arria, Helvidius Priscus, Annæus Cornutus, and Musonius Rufus, admirable masters of aristocratic virtue. The rigidity and exaggeration of this school arose from the horrible cruelty of the Cæsars. The continual thought of a good man was how to inure himself to suffering, and prepare himself for death. Lucian, in bad taste, and Persius with superior talent, but gave utterance to the loftiest sentiments of a great soul. Seneca the philosopher, Pliny the Elder, and Papirius Fabianus kept up a high standard of science and philosophy. Every one did not yield; there were a few wise men left. Too often, however, they had no resource but death. The ignoble portions of humanity at times got the upper hand. Then madness and cruelty ruled the hour, and made of Rome a veritable hell.

The government, altho so fearfully unstable at Rome, was much better in the provinces. At a distance the shocks which agitated the capital were hardly felt. In spite of its defects, the Roman administration was far superior to the kingdoms and commonwealths it had supplanted. The time for sovereign municipalities had long gone by. Those little states had destroyed themselves by their egotism, their jealousies, and their ignorance or neglect of individual freedom. The ancient life of Greece, all struggle, all external, no longer satisfied any one. It had been glorious in its day, but that brilliant democratic Olympus of demigods had lost its freshness, and become dry, cold, unmeaning, vain, superficial, and lacking in both head and heart. Hence the success of the Macedonian rule, and afterward of the Roman. The empire had not yet fallen into the error of excessive centralization. Until the time of Diocletian, the provinces and cities enjoyed much liberty. Kingdoms almost independent existed in Palestine, Syria, Asia Minor, Lesser Armenia, and Thrace, under the protection of Rome. These kingdoms became factions after Caligula only because the profound policy of Augustus concerning them was diverged from in succeeding reigns.

The numerous free cities were governed according to their own laws, and had the legislative power and magistracy of autonomic states. Until the third century their municipal decree commenced with the formula, "The Senate and People of—". The theaters were not simply placed for scenic amusement, but were foci of opinion and discussion. Most of the towns were, in different ways, little commonwealths. The municipal spirit was very strong. They had lost only the power to declare war, a fatal power which made the world a field of carnage. "The benefits conferred by Rome upon mankind" were the theme of adulatory addresses everywhere, to which, however, it would be unjust to deny some sincerity. The doctrine of "the Peace of Rome," the idea of a vast democracy organized under Roman protection, lay at the bottom of all political speculations. A Greek rhetorician displays vast erudition in proving that Roman glory should be claimed by all the branches of the Hellenic race as a common patrimony. In regard to Syria, Asia Minor, and Egypt, we may say that the Roman conquest did not destroy any of their liberties. Those nations had either been already long dead to political life, or had never enjoyed it.

Finally, in spite of the extortions of governors and of the violence which is inseparable from despotic sway, the world had in many respects never been so well off. An administration coming from a remote center was so great an advantage, that even the rapacious prætors of the latter days of the republic had failed to render it unpopular.

The Julian law had also narrowed down the scope of abuses and peculations. The follies or cruelties of the emperor, except under Nero, reached only the Roman aristocracy and the immediate followers of the prince. Never had men who did not care to busy themselves about politics been able to live more at ease. The ancient republics, in which every one was compelled to take part in the factions, were very uncomfortable places of residence. There was continually going on some disorganization or proscription. But under the empire the time seemed made expressly for great proselytism which should overrule both the quarrels of neighborhoods and the rivalry of dynasties. Attacks on liberty were much more frequently owing to the remnants of the provincial or communal authority than to the Roman administration. Of this truth we have had and shall have many occasions to take note.

For those of the conquered countries where political privileges had been unknown for ages, and which lost nothing but the right of destroying themselves by continual wars, the empire was such an era of prosperity and well-being as they had never before experienced; and we may add, without being paradoxical, that it was also for them an era of liberty. On the one hand, a freedom of commerce and industry, of which the Grecian state had no conception, became possible. On the other hand, the new régime could not but be favorable to freedom of thought. This freedom is always greater under a monarchy than under the rule of jealous and narrow-minded citizens, and it was unknown in the ancient republics. The Greeks accomplished great things without it, thanks to the incomparable force of their genius; but we must not forget that Athens had a complete inquisition. . . .

There was, indeed, under the empire more than one arbitrary decree against the philosophers, but it was always called forth by their entering into political schemes. We may search in vain the Roman law before Constantine for a single passage against freedom of thought; and the history of the imperial government furnishes no instance of a prosecution for entertaining an abstract doctrine. No scientific man was molested. Men like Galen, Lucan, and Plotinus, who would have gone to the stake in the Middle Age, lived tranquilly under the protection of the law. The empire inaugurated liberty in this respect; it extinguished the despotic sovereignty of the family, the town, and the tribe, and replaced or tempered it by that of the state. But despotic power is the more vexatious the narrower its sphere of action. The old republics and the feudal system opprest individuals much more than did the state. The empire at times persecuted Christianity most severely, but at least it did not arrest its progress. Republics, however, would have overcome the new faith. Even Judaism would have smothered it but for the pressure of Roman authority. The Roman magistrates were all that hindered the Pharisees from destroying Christianity at the outset.

HIPPOLITE ADOLPHE TAINE

Born in 1828, died in 1893; studied medicine and in taking his degree produced as a dissertation his notable "Essai sur les Fables de La Fontaine"; published other essays on Livy, Carlyle, and Mill; professor of esthetics at the École des Beaux Arts in 1864; published a book on the Pyrenees in 1855, one on Italy in 1866, and one on England 1872; his "History of English Literature," his masterpiece, published in 1864-65; "Les Origines de la France Contemporaine" 1875-90; elected to the French Academy in 1878.

I

THACKERAY AS A SATIRIST[1]

THE novel of manners in England multiplies, and for this there are several reasons: first, it is born there, and every plant thrives well in its own soil; secondly, it is a natural outlet: there is no music in England as in Germany, or conversation as in France; and men who must think and feel find in it a means of feeling and thinking. On the other hand, women take part in it with eagerness; amidst the stagnation of gallantry and the coldness of religion, it gives scope for imagination and dreams. Finally, by its minute details and practical counsels, it opens up a career to the precise and moral mind. The critic thus is, as it were, swamped in this copiousness; he must select in order to grasp the whole,

[1] From Book V, Chapter II of "The History of English Literature." Translated by H. van Laun.

and confine himself to a few in order to embrace all.

In this crowd two men have appeared of superior talent, original and contrasted, popular on the same grounds, ministers to the same cause, moralists in comedy and drama, defenders of natural sentiments against social institutions; who, by the precision of their pictures, the depth of their observations, the succession and bitterness of their attacks, have renewed, with other views and in another style, the old combative spirit of Swift and Fielding.

One, more ardent, more expansive, wholly given up to rapture, an impassioned painter of crude and dazzling pictures, a lyric prose-writer, omnipotent in laughter and tears, plunged into fantastic invention, painful sensibility, vehement buffoonery; and by the boldness of his style, the excess of his emotions, the grotesque familiarity of his caricatures, he has displayed all the forces and weaknesses of an artist, all the audacities, all the successes, and all the oddities of the imagination.

The other, more contained, better informed and stronger, a lover of moral dissertations, a counselor of the public, a sort of lay preacher, less bent on defending the poor, more bent on censuring man, has brought to the aid of satire a sustained common sense, a great knowledge of the heart, consummate cleverness, powerful reasoning, a treasure of meditated hatred, and has persecuted vice with all the weapons of reflection. By this contrast the one completes the other; and we may form an exact idea of English taste, by placing the portrait of William Makepeace

Thackeray by the side of that of Charles Dickens.

No wonder if in England a novelist writes satires. A gloomy and reflective man is impelled to it by his character; he is still further impelled by the surrounding manners. He is not permitted to contemplate passions as poetic powers; he is bidden to appreciate them as moral qualities. His pictures become sentences; he is a counselor rather than an observer, a judge rather than an artist. We see by what machinery Thackeray has changed novel into satire. . . .

Who is he; and what is the value of this literature of which he is one of the princes? At bottom, like every literature, it is a definition of man; and to judge it, we must compare it with man. We can do so now; we have just studied a mind, Thackeray himself; we have considered his faculties, their connections, results, their different degrees; we have before our eyes a model of human nature. We have a right to judge of the copy by the model, and to control the definition which his novels lay down by the definition which his character furnishes.

The two definitions are contrary, and his portrait is a criticism on his talent. We have seen that in him the same faculties produce the beautiful and the ugly, force and weakness, success and failure; that moral reflection, after having provided him with every satirical power, debases him in art; that, after having spread over his contemporary novels a tone of vulgarity and falseness, it raises his historical novel to the level of the finest productions; that the same constitution of mind teaches him the sarcastic and violent, as well as the modulated and simple style, the bitterness and harshness of hate with the effusion and delicacy of love. The evil and the good, the beautiful and the ugly, the repulsive and the agreeable, are in him then but remoter effects, of slight importance, born of changing circumstances, acquired and fortuitous qualities, not essential and primitive, different forms which different streams present in the same current.

So it is with other men. Doubtless moral qualities are of the first rank; they are the motive power of civilization, and constitute the nobleness of the individual; society exists by them alone, and by them alone man is great. But if they are the finest fruit of the human plant, they are not its root; they give us our value, but do not constitute our elements. Neither the vices nor the virtues of man are his nature; to praise or to blame him is not to know him; approbation or disapprobation does not define him; the names of good or bad tell us nothing of what he is. Put the robber Cartouche in an Italian court of the fifteenth century; he would be a great statesman. Transport this nobleman, stingy and narrow-minded, into a shop; he will be an exemplary tradesman. This public man, of inflexible probity, is in his drawing-room an intolerable coxcomb. This father of a family, so humane, is an idiotic politician. Change a virtue in its circumstances, and it becomes a vice; change a vice in its circumstances, and it becomes a virtue. Regard the same quality from two sides; on one it is a fault, on the other a merit. The essential man is found concealed far below these moral badges; they only point out the useful or noxious effect of our inner constitution: they do not reveal our inner constitution. They are safety or advertising lights attached to our names, to warn the passer-by to avoid or approach us; they are not the explanatory chart of our being.

Our true essence consists in the causes of our good or bad qualities, and these causes are discovered in the temperament, the species and degree of imagination, the amount and velocity of attention, the magnitude and direction of primitive passions. A character is a force, like gravity, or steam, capable, as it may happen, of pernicious or profitable effects, and which must be defined otherwise than by the amount of the weight it can lift or the havoc it can cause. It is therefore to ignore man, to reduce him, as Thackeray and English literature generally do, to an aggregate of virtues and vices; it is to lose sight in him of all but the exterior and social side; it is to neglect the inner and natural element. We will find the same fault in English criticism, always moral, never psychological, bent on exactly measuring the degree of human honesty, ignorant of the mechanism of our sentiments and faculties; we will find the same fault in English religion, which is but an emotion or a discipline; in their philosophy, destitute of metaphysics; and if we ascend to the source, according to the rule which derives vices from virtues, and virtues from vices, we will see all these weaknesses derived from their native energy, their practical education, and that kind of severe and religious poetic instinct which has in time past made them Protestant and Puritan.

II

WHEN THE KING GOT UP FOR THE DAY[2]

THE king is expected to keep the entire aristocracy busy; consequently, to make a display of himself, to pay back with his own person, at all hours even the most private, even on getting out of bed, and even in his bed. In the morning, at the hour named by himself beforehand, the head valet awakens him; five series of persons enter in turn to perform their duty, and, "altho very large, there are days when the waiting-rooms can hardly contain the crowd of courtiers." The first one admitted is "l'entrée familière," consisting of the children of France, the prince and princesses of the blood, and besides these, the chief physician, the chief surgeon, and other serviceable persons. Next comes the "grande entrée," which comprizes the grand chamberlain, the grand master and master of the wardrobe, the first gentlemen of the bedchamber, the dukes of Orleans and Penthièvre, some other highly favored seigniors, the ladies of honor and in waiting of the queen, mesdames, and other princesses, without enumerating barbers, tailors, and various descriptions of valets. Meanwhile spirits of wine are poured on the king's hands from a service of plate, and he is then handed the basin of holy-water; he crosses himself and repeats a prayer.

Then he gets out of bed before all these people,

[2] From "The Ancient Régime." Translated by John Durand. Copyright, 1876, by Henry Holt & Company.

and puts on his slippers. The grand chamberlain and the first gentleman hand him his dressing-gown; he puts this on and seats himself in the chair in which he is to put on his clothes. At this moment the door opens, and a third group enters, which is the "entrée des brevets"—the seigniors who compose this enjoy in addition the precious privilege of assisting at the "petit coucher"; while at the same moment there enters a detachment of attendants, consisting of the physicians and surgeons in ordinary, the intendants of the amusements, readers, and others, and among the latter those who preside over physical requirements. The publicity of a royal life is so great that none of its functions can be exercised without witnesses.

At the moment of the approach of the officers of the wardrobe to dress the king, the first gentleman, notified by an usher, advances to read him the names of the grandees who are waiting at the door: this is the fourth entry, called "la chambre," and larger than those preceding it; for, not to mention the cloak-bearers, gun-bearers, rug-bearers, and other valets, it comprizes most of the superior officials, the grand almoner, the almoners on duty, the chaplain, the master of the oratory, the captain and major of the bodyguard, the colonel-general and major of the French guards, the colonel of the king's regiment, the captain of the *Cent Suisses*, the grand huntsman, the grand wolf-huntsman, the grand provost, the grand master and master of ceremonies, the first butler, the grand master of the pantry, the foreign ambassadors, the ministers and secretaries of state, the marshals of France, and most of the seigniors and prelates of distinction. Ushers place the ranks in order, and if necessary, impose silence.

Meanwhile the king washes his hands and begins his toilet. Two pages remove his slippers; the grand master of the wardrobe draws off his night-shirt by the right arm, and the first valet of the wardrobe by the left arm, and both of them hand it to an officer of the wardrobe, while a valet of the wardrobe fetches the shirt, wrapt up in white taffeta. Things have now reached the solemn point, the culmination of the ceremony: the fifth entry has been introduced; and in a few moments, after the king has put his shirt on, all that is left of those who are known, with other household officers waiting in the gallery, complete the influx.

There is quite a formality in regard to this shirt. The honor of handing it is reserved to the sons and grandsons of France; in default of these, to the princes of the blood or those legitimated; in their default, to the grand chamberlain or to the first gentleman of the bedchamber; the latter case, it must be observed, being very rare, the princes being obliged to be present at the king's *lever* as well as the princesses at that of the queen. At last the shirt is presented, and a valet carries off the old one; the first valet of the wardrobe and the first valet de chambre hold the fresh one, each by a right and left arm respectively; while two other valets, during this operation, extend his dressing-gown in front of him to serve as a screen. The shirt is now on his back, and the toilet commences.

A valet de chambre supports a mirror before

the king, while two others on the two sides light it up, if occasion requires with flambeaux. Valets of the wardrobe fetch the rest of the attire; the grand master of the wardrobe puts the vest on and the doublet, attaches the blue ribbon, and clasps his sword around him; then a valet assigned to the cravats brings several of these in a basket, while the master of the wardrobe arranges around the king's neck that which the king selects. After this a valet assigned to the handkerchiefs brings three of these on a silver salver; while the grand master of the wardrobe offers the salver to the king, who chooses one. Finally the master of the wardrobe hands to the king his hat, his gloves, and his cane. The king then steps to the side of the bed, kneels on a cushion, and says his prayers; while an almoner in a low voice recites the orison *Quæsumus, deus omnipotens*. This done, the king announces the order of the day, and passes with the leading persons of his court into his cabinet, where he sometimes gives audience. Meanwhile the rest of the company await him in the gallery, in order to accompany him to mass when he comes out.

Such is the *lever*, a piece in five acts. Nothing could be contrived better calculated to fill up the void of an aristocratic life: a hundred or thereabouts of notable seigniors dispose of a couple of hours in coming, in waiting, in entering, in defiling, in taking positions, in standing on their feet, in maintaining an air of respect and of ease suitable to a superior class of walking gentlemen, while those best qualified are about to do the same thing over in the queen's apartment. The king, however, to offset this, suffers the same torture and the same inaction as he imposes. He also is playing a part: all his steps and all his gestures have been determined beforehand; he has been obliged to arrange his physiognomy and his voice, never to depart from an affable and dignified air, to award judiciously his glances and his nods, to keep silent or to speak only of the chase, and to suppress his own thoughts if he has any. One can not indulge in reverie, meditate, or be absent-minded when before the footlights: the part must have due attention.

EMILE ZOLA

Born in 1840, died in 1902; his father an Italian, his
mother French; became a packing clerk in a bookstore in
1860; published his first book in 1864; "L'Assommoir" in
1877, "Nana" in 1880, "La Terre" in 1887, author of many
other works; prominent in the Dreyfus case, being twice
fined and imprisoned for libeling a court martial.

GLIMPSES OF NAPOLEON III IN TIME OF WAR [1]

THEY had no more than sat down at table when
Delaherche, burning to relieve himself of the subject that filled his mind, began to relate his ex-
periences of the day before.

"You know I saw the Emperor at Baybel."

He was fairly started, and nothing could stop
him. He began by describing the farmhouse;
a large structure with an interior court, surrounded by an iron railing, and situated on a
gentle eminence overlooking Mouzon, to the left
of the Carignan road. Then he came back to
the Twelfth Corps, whom he had visited in their
camp among the vines on the hillsides; splendid
troops they were, with their equipments brightly
shining in the sunlight, and the sight of them
had caused his heart to beat with patriotic ardor.

"And there I was, sir, when the Emperor, who
had alighted to breakfast and rest himself a bit,

[1] From "La Débâcle." Translated by E. P. Robins.
Copyright, 1892, by Cassell Publishing Company. Copyright,
1898, by the Macmillan Company.

came out of the farmhouse. He wore a general's uniform and carried an overcoat across his arm, altho the sun was very hot. He was followed by a servant bearing a camp-stool. He did not look to me like a well man; ah no, far from it: his stooping form, the sallowness of his complexion, the feebleness of his movements, all indicated him to be in a very bad way. I was not surprized; for the druggist at Mouzon, when he recommended me to drive on to Baybel, told me that an aide-de-camp had just been in his shop to get some medicine—you understand what I mean—medicine for—''

The presence of his wife and mother prevented him from alluding more explicitly to the nature of the Emperor's complaint, which was an obstinate diarrhea that he had contracted at Chêne, and which compelled him to make those frequent halts at houses along the road.

''Well, then the attendant opened the camp-stool and placed it in the shade of a clump of trees at the edge of a field of wheat, and the Emperor sat down on it. Sitting there in a limp, dejected attitude, perfectly still, he looked for all the world like a small shopkeeper taking a sun-bath for his rheumatism. His dull eyes wandered over the wide horizon, the Meuse coursing through the valley at his feet, before him the range of wooded heights whose summits recede and are lost in the distance, on the left the waving tree-tops of Dieulet forest, on the right the verdure-clad eminence of Sommanthe. He was surrounded by his military family, aides and officers of rank; and a colonel of dragoons, who had already applied to me for information about the country, had just motioned me not to go away, when all at once—''

Delaherche rose from his chair, for he had reached the point where the dramatic interest of his story culminated, and it became necessary to reenforce words by gestures.

''All at once there was a succession of sharp reports; and right in front of us, over the wood of Dieulet, shells are seen circling through the air. It produced on me no more effect than a display of fireworks in broad daylight, sir, upon my word it didn't! The people about the Emperor, of course, showed a good deal of agitation and uneasiness. The colonel of dragoons comes running up again to ask if I can give them an idea whence the fire proceeds. I answer him offhand: 'It is at Beaumont; there is not the slightest doubt about it.' He returns to the Emperor, on whose knees an aide-de-camp was unfolding a map. The Emperor was evidently of opinion that the fighting was not at Beaumont, for he sent the colonel back to me a third time. But I couldn't well do otherwise than stick to what I had said before, could I, now?—the more that the shells kept flying through the air, nearer and nearer, following the line of the Mouzon road. And then, sir, as sure as I see you standing there, I saw the Emperor turn his pale face toward me. Yes, sir, he looked at me a moment with those dim eyes of his, that were filled with an expression of melancholy and distrust. And then his face declined upon his map again, and he made no further movement.''

Delaherche, altho he was an ardent Bonapartist at the time of the plébiscite, had admitted after our early defeats that the government was responsible for some mistakes; but he stood up for the dynasty, compassionating and excusing Napoleon III, deceived and betrayed as he was by every one. It was his firm opinion that the men at whose door should be laid the responsibility for all our disasters were none other than those Republican deputies of the opposition who had stood in the way of voting the necessary men and money.

"And did the Emperor return to the farmhouse?" asked Captain Beaudoin.

"That's more than I can say, my dear sir: I left him sitting on his stool. It was midday, the battle was drawing nearer, and it occurred to me that it was time to be thinking of my own return. All that I can tell you besides is that a general to whom I pointed out the position of Carignan in the distance, in the plain to our rear, appeared greatly surprised to learn that the Belgian frontier lay in that direction, and was only a few miles away. Ah, that the poor Emperor should have to rely on such servants!" . . .

While Delaherche was raising himself on tiptoe, and trying to peer through the windows of the *rez-de-chaussée*, an old woman at his side, some poor day-worker of the neighborhood, with shapeless form, and hands calloused and distorted by many years of toil, was mumbling between her teeth:

"An emperor—I should like to see one once— just once—so I could say I had seen him."

Suddenly Delaherche exclaimed, seizing Maurice by the arm:

"See, there he is! at the window to the left. I had a good view of him yesterday; I can't be mistaken. There, he has just raised the curtain; see, that pale face, close to the glass."

The old woman had overheard him, and stood staring with wide-open mouth and eyes; for there, full in the window, was an apparition that resembled a corpse more than a living being: its eyes were lifeless, its features distorted; even the mustache had assumed a ghastly whiteness in the final agony. The old woman was dumfounded; forthwith she turned her back and marched off with a look of supreme contempt.

"That thing an emperor! a likely story!"

A zouave was standing near—one of those fugitive soldiers who were in no haste to rejoin their commands. Brandishing his chassepot and expectorating threats and maledictions, he said to his companion:

"Wait! see me put a bullet in his head!"

Delaherche remonstrated angrily; but by that time the Emperor had disappeared. The hoarse murmur of the Meuse continued uninterruptedly; a wailing lament, inexpressibly mournful, seemed to pass above them through the air, where the darkness was gathering intensity. Other sounds rose in the distance, like the hollow muttering of the rising storm: were they the "March! march!"—that terrible order from Paris which had driven that ill-starred man onward day by day, dragging behind him along the roads of his defeat the irony of his imperial escort, until now he was brought face to face with the ruin he had foreseen and come forth to meet? What multitudes of brave men were to lay down their lives for his mistakes; and how complete the wreck, in all his being, of that sick man—that sentimental dreamer, awaiting in gloomy silence the fulfilment of his destiny! . . .

"O M. Delaherche! isn't this dreadful! Here, quick! this way, if you would like to see the Emperor."

On the left of the corridor a door stood ajar; and through the narrow opening a glimpse could be had of the sovereign, who had resumed his weary, anguished tramp between the fireplace and the window. Back and forth he shuffled with heavy, dragging steps, and ceased not, despite his unendurable suffering. An aide-de-camp had just entered the room—it was he who had failed to close the door behind him—and Delaherche heard the Emperor ask him in a sorrowfully reproachful voice:

"What is the reason of this continued firing, sir, after I gave orders to hoist the white flag?"

The torture to him had become greater than he could bear—this never-ceasing cannonade that seemed to grow more furious with every minute. Every time he approached the window it pierced him to the heart. More spilling of blood, more useless squandering of human life! At every moment the piles of corpses were rising higher on the battle-field, and his was the responsibility. The compassionate instincts that entered so largely into his nature revolted at it, and more than ten times already he had asked that question of those who approached him.

"I gave orders to raise the white flag: tell me, why do they continue firing?"

The aide-de-camp made answer in a voice so

low that Delaherche failed to catch its purport. The Emperor, moreover, seemed not to pause to listen, drawn by some irresistible attraction to that window; at which, each time he approached it, he was greeted by that terrible salvo of artillery that rent and tore his being. His pallor was greater even than it had been before; his poor, pinched, wan face, on which were still visible traces of the rouge which had been applied that morning, bore witness to his anguish.

At that moment a short, quick-motioned man in dust-soiled uniform, whom Delaherche recognized as General Lebrun, hurriedly crossed the corridor and pushed open the door, without waiting to be announced. And scarcely was he in the room when again was heard the Emperor's so oft-repeated question.

"Why do they continue to fire, General, when I have given orders to hoist the white flag?"

The aide-de-camp left the apartment, shutting the door behind him, and Delaherche never knew what was the General's answer. The vision had faded from his sight.

ALPHONSE DAUDET

Born in 1840, died in 1897; educated at Lyons; settled in Paris in 1857 and began to write poems and sketches for newspapers and periodicals; his "Fromont Jeune et Risler Ainé" published in 1874, "Jack" in 1876, "Numa Roume-stan" in 1881, "Tartarin sur les Alps" in 1885; author of many other works of fiction.

I

A GREAT MAN'S WIDOW [1]

No one was astonished at hearing she was going to marry again. Notwithstanding all his genius, perhaps even on account of his genius, the great man had for fifteen years led her a hard life, full of caprices and mad freaks that had attracted the attention of all Paris. On the highroad to fame, over which he had so triumphantly and hurriedly traveled, like those who are to die young, she had sat behind him, humbly and tim-idly, in a corner of the chariot, ever fearful of collisions. Whenever she complained, relatives, friends, every one was against her: "Respect his weaknesses," they would say to her, "they are the weaknesses of a god. Do not disturb him, do not worry him. Remember that your husband does not belong exclusively to you. He belongs much more to art, to his country, than to his family. And who knows if each of the faults you reproach him with has not given us

[1] From "Artists' Wives." Translated by Laura Ensor.

55

some sublime creation?'' At last, however, her patience was worn out, she rebelled, became indignant and even unjust, so much, indeed, that at the moment of the great man's death, they were on the point of demanding a judicial separation and ready to see their great and celebrated name dragged into the columns of a society paper.

After the agitation of this unhappy match, the anxieties of the last illness, and the sudden death which for a moment revived her former affection, the first months of her widowhood acted on the young woman like a healthy calming water-cure. The enforced retirement, the quiet charm of mitigated sorrow lent to her thirty-five years a second youth almost as attractive as the first.

Moreover, black suited her, and then she had the responsible and rather proud look of a woman left alone in life, with all the weight of a great name to carry honorably. Mindful of the fame of the departed one, that wretched fame that had cost her so many tears, and now grew day by day, like a magnificent flower nourished by the black earth of the tomb, she was to be seen draped in her long somber veils holding interviews with theatrical managers and publishers, busying herself in getting her husband's operas put again on the stage, superintending the printing of his posthumous works and unfinished manuscripts, bestowing on all these details a kind of solemn care and, as it were, the respect for a shrine.

It was at this moment that her second husband met her. He, too, was a musician, almost unknown, it is true, the author of a few waltzes and songs, and of two little operas, of which the scores, charmingly printed, were scarcely more played than sold. With a pleasant countenance, a handsome fortune that he owed to his exceedingly bourgeois family, he had above all an infinite respect for genius, a curiosity about famous men, and the ingenuous enthusiasm of a still youthful artist. Thus when he met the wife of the great man, he was dazzled and bewildered. It was as tho the image of the glorious muse herself had appeared to him. He at once fell in love, and as the widow was beginning to receive a few friends, he had himself presented to her. There his passion grew in the atmosphere of genius that still lingered in all the corners of the drawing-room. There was the bust of the master, the piano he composed on, his scores spread over all the furniture, melodious even to look at, as tho from between their half-opened pages the written phrases reechoed musically. The actual and very real charm of the widow, surrounded by those austere memories as by a frame that became her, brought his love to a climax.

After hesitating a long time, the poor fellow at last proposed, but in such humble and timid terms: "He knew how unworthy he was of her. He understood all the regret she would feel in exchanging her illustrious name for his, so unknown and insignificant." And a thousand other artless phrases in the same style. In reality, the lady was indeed very much flattered by her conquest; however, she played the comedy of a broken heart, and assumed the disdainful, wearied airs of a woman whose life is ended without hopes of renewal. She, who had never in her life been so quiet and comfortable as since the death of her great man, actually found tears with which to mourn for him, and an enthusiastic ardor in speaking of him. This, of course, only inflamed her youthful adorer the more and made him more eloquent and persuasive.

In short, this severe widowhood ended in a marriage; but the widow did not abdicate, and remained — altho married — more than ever the widow of a great man; well knowing that herein lay, in the eyes of her second husband, her real prestige. As she felt herself much older than he, to prevent his perceiving it, she overwhelmed him with her disdain, with a kind of vague pity, and unexprest and offensive regret at her condescending marriage. However, he was not wounded by it, quite the contrary. He was so convinced of his inferiority and thought it so natural that the memory of such a man should reign despotically in her heart! In order the better to maintain in him this humble attitude, she would at times read over with him the letters the great man had written to her when he was courting her. This return toward the past rejuvenated her some fifteen years, lent her the assurance of a handsome and beloved woman, seen through all the wild love and delightful exaggeration of written passion. That she since then had changed her young husband cared little, loving her on the faith of another, and drawing therefrom I know not what strange kind of vanity. It seemed to him that these passionate appeals added to his own, and that he inherited a whole past of love.

A strange couple indeed! It was in society,

however, that they presented the most curious spectacle. I sometimes caught sight of them at the theater. No one would have recognized the timid and shy young woman, who formerly accompanied the maestro, lost in the gigantic shadow he cast around him. Now, seated upright in the front of the box, she displayed herself, attracting all eyes by the pride of her own glance. It might be said that her head was surrounded by her first husband's halo of glory, his name reechoing around her like a homage or a reproach. The other one, seated a little behind her, with the subservient physiognomy of one ready for every abnegation in life, watched each of her movements, ready to attend to her slightest wish.

At home the peculiarity of their attitude was still more noticeable. I remember a certain evening party they gave a year after their marriage. The husband moved about among the crowd of guests, proud but rather embarrassed at gathering together so many in his own house. The wife, disdainful, melancholy, and very superior, was on that evening more than ever the widow of a great man! She had a peculiar way of glancing at her husband from over her shoulder, of calling him "my poor dear friend," of casting on him all the wearisome drudgery of the reception, with an air of saying: "You are only fit for that." Around her gathered a circle of former friends, those who had been spectators of the brilliant débuts of the great man, of his struggles, and his success. She simpered to them; played the young girl! They had known her when so young! Nearly all of them called her

by her Christian name, "Anais." They formed
a kind of cœnaculum, which the poor husband
respectfully approached, to hear his predecessor
spoken of. They recalled the glorious first nights,
those evenings on which nearly every battle was
won, and the great man's manias, his way of
working; how, in order to summon up inspira-
tion, he insisted on his wife being by his side,
decked out in full ball dress. "Do you remember, Anais?" And Anais sighed and blushed.

It was at that time that he had written his
most tender pieces, above all "Savonarole," the
most passionate of his creations, with a grand
duet, interwoven with rays of moonshine, the
perfume of roses and the warbling of nightingales. An enthusiast sat down and played it on
the piano, amid a silence of attentive emotion.
At the last note of the magnificent piece, the
lady burst into tears. "I can not help it," she
said, "I have never been able to hear it without
weeping." The great man's old friends surrounded his unhappy widow with sympathetic
expressions, coming up to her one by one, as
at a funereal ceremony, to give a thrilling clasp
to her hand.

"Come, come, Anais, be courageous." And
the drollest thing was to see the second husband,
standing by the side of his wife, deeply touched
and affected, shaking hands all round, and accepting, he too, his share of sympathy. "What
genius! what genius!" he repeated as he mopped
his eyes. It was at the same time ridiculous and
affecting.

ALPHONSE DAUDET

MY FIRST DRESS COAT [2]

How did I come by it, that first dress coat?
What primitive tailor, what confiding tradesman
was it, trustful as Don Juan's famous Monsieur
Dimanche, who upon the faith of my fantastic
promises, decided one fine morning on bringing
it to me, brand new, and artistically pinned up
in a square of shiny green calico? It would be
difficult for me to tell. Of the honest tailor, I
can indeed recall nothing—so many tailors have
since then crossed my path—save perhaps a
vision, as in a luminous mist, of a thoughtful
brow and a large mustache. The coat indeed is
there, before my eyes. Its image after twenty
years still remains indelibly graven on my memory, as on imperishable brass. What a collar, my
young friends! What lapels! And, above all,
what skirts, shaped as the slimmest tail of the
swallow! My brother, a man of experience, had
said: "One must have a dress coat if one wishes
to make one's way in the world." And the dear
fellow counted much upon this piece of frippery
for the advancement of my fame and fortune. . . .

One day some one proposed to get me an in-
vitation to Augustine Brohan's soirées. Who?
some one. Some one, egad! You know him
already: that eternal some one, who is like every

[2] From "Thirty Years of Paris." Translated by Laura Ensor.

one else, that amiable institution of Providence, who, of no personal value in himself and a mere acquaintance in the house he frequents, yet goes everywhere, introduces you everywhere, is the friend of a day, of an hour, of whose name even you are ignorant, that essentially Parisian type.

You may imagine with what enthusiasm I accepted the proposal. To be invited to Augustine's house! Augustine, the famous actress, Augustine, the laughing representative of Molière's comic muse, softened somewhat by the more modern poetic smile of Musset's genius — for while she acted the waiting maids at the Théâtre Français, Musset had written his comedy "Louison" at her house; Augustine Brohan, in short, in whom all Paris delighted, vaunting her wit, quoting her repartees; and who might already be said to have adorned herself with that swallow's plume, unsullied yet by ink, but already well sharpened, with which she was hereafter to sign those charming "Lettres de Suzanne!"

"Lucky dog!" said my brother, helping me on with the coat; "your fortune is made."

Nine o'clock was striking as I sallied forth.

At that time Augustine Brohan was living in the Rue Lord Byron, at the top of the Champs Élysées, in one of those pretty coquettish little houses which seem to ignorant provincials the realization of the poetical dreams which they weave for themselves from the pages of the novelist. A railing, a tiny garden, four steps covered by an awning, an entrance hall filled with flowers, and then, opening immediately from it, the drawing-room, a brilliantly lighted room in green, which I can see now vividly before me.

How I managed to get up those steps, how I made my entry, and how I presented myself, I can not now remember. A footman announced my name, but this name, which he mumbled, produced no effect on the brilliant assembly. I can only recollect hearing a woman's voice say: "So much the better, here is another dancer." It appears they were short of dancers; but what an entry for a poet!

Startled and humiliated, I tried to lose myself among the crowd. How can I describe my dismay, when, a moment later, another mistake arose? My long hair, my dark and somber looks excited general curiosity. I heard them whispering near me: "Who is it? Do look," and they laughed. At last some one said:

"It is the Wallachian Prince!"

"The Wallachian Prince? Oh yes, very likely."

I suppose that a Wallachian prince had been expected that evening. My rank being thus settled for me, I was left in peace. But for all that, you can not imagine how heavily my usurped crown weighed upon me all that evening. First a dancing man! then a Wallachian prince! Could not these good people see my lyre?

Fortunately for me, a startling piece of news flying from mouth to mouth, spread rapidly through the ballroom, casting into oblivion both the dancer and the Wallachian prince. Marriage was at that time much the fashion among the feminine portion of the Comédie company, and it was generally at Augustine Brohan's Wednesday receptions, where all the choicest talents of journalism, together with bankers and high government officials gathered round the lovely members or associates of the Français, that the foundations were laid of most of these romantic unions. . . .

At last comparative calm was restored and the quadrilles began. I danced. I was obliged to do so. I danced moreover somewhat badly for a Wallachian prince. The quadrille once ended, I became stationary; foolishly held back by my short sight—too shy to sport an eyeglass, too much of a poet to wear spectacles, and dreading lest, at the slightest movement, I should bruise my knee against the corner of some piece of furniture, or plunge my nose into the trimming of a bodice. Soon hunger and thirst interfered in the matter; but for a kingdom I should never have dared to approach the buffet with all the rest of the world. I anxiously watched for the moment when it should be deserted; and while waiting, I joined the groups of political talkers, assuming a serious air, and feigning to scorn the charms of the smaller salon, whence came to me, with the pleasant sound of laughter and the tinkling of teaspoons against the porcelain, a delicate aroma of scented tea, of Spanish wines and cakes. At last they came back to dance, and I gathered up my courage. I entered, I was alone.

What a dazzling sight was that buffet. A crystal pyramid under the blaze of the candles, brilliant with glasses and decanters, white and glittering as snow in the sunshine. I took up a glass as fragile as a flower, careful not to hold it too tightly lest I should break the stem. What should I pour into it? Come now, courage, I say to myself, since no one can see me. I stretched out my hand, and took at haphazard a decanter. It must be kirsch, I thought, from its diamond clearness. Well, I'll try a glass of kirsch; I like its perfume, its bitter and wild perfume that reminds me of the forest. And so, like an epicure, I slowly poured out, drop by drop, the beautiful clear liquid. I raised the glass to my lips. Oh, horror, it was only water. What a grimace I made. Suddenly a duet of laughter resounded from a black coat and a pink dress that I had not perceived flirting in the corner, and who were amused at my mistake.

I endeavored to replace my glass, but I was nervous, my hand shook, and my sleeve caught I know not what. One glass, two glasses, three glasses fell. I turned round, my wretched coat tails swept a wild circle, and the white pyramid crashed to the ground, with all the sparkling, splintering, flashing uproar of an iceberg breaking to pieces.

At the noise of the catastrophe the mistress of the house rushed up. Luckily, she is as short-sighted as the Wallachian prince, and he is able to escape from the buffet without being recognized. All the same, my evening is spoiled. The massacre of small glasses and decanters weighs on my mind like a crime. My one idea is to get away. But the Dubois mama, dazzled by my principality, catches hold of me and will not allow me to leave till I have danced with her daughter, or indeed with both her daughters. I excuse myself as best as I can; when a tall old man with a shrewd smile, stopt my egress. It is Doctor Ricord, with whom I had exchanged a few words previously and who, like the others, takes me for the Wallachian. "But, Prince, as you are inhabiting the Hotel du Senat, and as we are near neighbors, pray wait for me, I can offer you a seat in my carriage." How willingly would I accept, but I have no overcoat. What would Ricord think of a Wallachian prince without furs, and shivering in his dress coat? Let me escape quickly, and hurry home on foot, through the snow and fog, sooner than allow my poverty to be seen. Always half-blind and more confused than ever, I reach the door and slip out, not, however, without getting somehow entangled in the tapestries. "Won't monsieur take his coat?" a footman calls after me.

There I was, at two o'clock in the morning, far from my home, alone in the streets, hungry and frozen, with the devil's own self, a badly lined purse in my pocket. But hunger inspired me with a brilliant idea: "Suppose I go to the markets." I had often heard of the markets, and a certain Gaidras, whose establishment remained open all night, and where for the sum of three sous they provided a plateful of succulent cabbage soup. By Jove, yes, to the markets I would go. I would sit down at those tables like the veriest prowling vagabond. All my pride had vanished. The wind is icy cold; hunger makes me desperate. "My kingdom for a horse," said another prince, and I say to myself as I trot along: "My principality, my Wallachian principality, for a basin of good soup in a warm corner."

Gaidras' establishment looks a mere filthy hovel, all slimy and badly lighted, thrust back beneath the colonnades of the old market-place. Often and often since then, when noctambulism was the fashion, have we, future great men, spent whole nights there, elbows on table, amidst tobacco smoke and literary talk. But at the first I must own, notwithstanding my hunger, I almost drew back at the sight of those blackened dingy walls, that dense smoke, those late sitters, snoring with their backs against the wall or lapping their soup like dogs; the amazing caps of the Don Juans of the gutter, the enormous drab felt hats of the market porters, and the healthy rough blouse of the market gardener side by side with the greasy tatters of the prowler of the night. Nevertheless I entered, and I may at once add that my black coat found its fellows. Black coats that own no great coat are not rare in Paris after midnight in the winter, and they are hungry enough to eat three sous' worth of cabbage soup. The cabbage soup was, however, exquisite; full of perfume as a garden, and smoking like a crater. I had two helpings, altho a custom peculiar to the establishment—inspired by wholesome distrust—of fastening the forks and spoons with a chain to the table, hindered me a little. I paid, and fortified by my substantial mess, resumed my way to the Quartier Latin.

What a picture my return home! The return of the poet, trotting up the Rue de Tournon, with his coat collar turned up, while dancing before his sleepy eyes are the elegant shadows of a fashionable evening party mingling with the famished specters of the market-place. He stands knocking his boots against the curbstone of the Hotel du Senat, to shake off the snow, while opposite the bright lamps of a brougham light up the front of an old mansion, and Doctor Ricord's coachman cries out: "Gate, if you please." Life in Paris is made up of these contrasts.

"A wasted evening," said my brother the next morning. "You have been taken for a Wallachian prince, and have not succeeded in launching your book. But all is not yet lost; you must make up for it when you make your 'digestion call,' as we say in Paris."

The digestion of a glass of water, what irony. It was quite two months before I made up my mind to pay that call. However, one day I summoned up courage. Besides her official receptions on Wednesdays, Augustine Brohan received more unceremoniously on Sunday afternoon. I resolutely started off. . . .

Even now I can recall the smallest details of that interview. But see how all depends upon our point of view. I had told Sarcey the comical story of my first appearance in society, and one day Sarcey repeated it to Augustine Brohan. Well, the ungrateful Augustine—whom, it is true, I have not seen for thirty years—swore most sincerely that she knew nothing of me but my books. She had forgotten everything! Everything—all that had played such an important part in my life—the broken glasses, the Wallachian prince, the rehearsal of "Lait d'Anesse," and the boots of the heavy dragoons.

GUY DE MAUPASSANT

Born in 1850, died in 1893; educated at Rouen; trained in literary matters by Flaubert; wrote an unsuccessful play in 1879 and then a short story, "Boule de Suif," which attracted marked attention, and was followed by a great number of short and long stories, including "Mademoiselle Fifi" in 1882, "Pierre et Jean" in 1888, and "Notre Cœur" in 1890.

MADAME JEANNE'S LAST DAYS [1]

JEANNE did not go out any more. She hardly bestirred herself. She got up every morning at the same time; looked out of the window at the weather, and then went down-stairs, and sat before the fire in the hall. Here she would think of the happy years of Paul's childhood, when he had worked in the salad-bed, kneeling side by side in the soft ground with Aunt Lison, the two women rivals in their effort to amuse the child, and seeing who could root up the young plants most skilfully.

So musing, her lips would murmur, "Poulet, Poulet! my little Poulet"—as if she were speaking to him; and, her reverie broken as she spoke, she would try during whole hours to write in the air the letters which formed the boy's name. She would trace them slowly before the fire, imagining that she really saw them; then believing that her eyes had deceived her, she would rewrite the

[1] From the last chapter of "A Life." Translated for this collection by Eric Arthur Bell.

capital P again, her arm trembling with fatigue, forcing herself to trace the name to the end; then when she had finished it she would begin over again. At last she could not write it any more. She would muddle everything—form other words, and exhaust herself almost to idiocy.

Ever since her childhood just one habit had clung to her—that of jumping up out of bed the moment she had drunk her morning coffee. She was inordinately fond of that way of breakfasting, and the privation would have been felt more than anything else. Each morning she would await Rosalie's arrival with extraordinary impatience; and as soon as the cup was put upon the table at her side, she would sit up and empty it almost greedily, and then, throwing off her robe, she would begin to dress herself at once.

She thought she was directly pursued by obstinate misfortune against which she became as fatalistic as an Oriental: the habit of seeing her dreams fade away and destroy her hopes made her afraid to undertake anything; and she waited whole days to accomplish the most simple affair, convinced that she would always take the wrong way to do it, and that it would turn out badly. She repeated continually, "I have never had any luck in my life." Then Rosalie would cry, "Supposing you had had to work for your bread—and were obliged to get up every morning at six o'clock and prepare for your day's doings? There are lots of people who are obliged to do that; and when such people become too old, they die of poverty."

She had checked certain memorable days in her life, and now and then she was able to remember episodes of an entire month, bringing them up one by one, grouping them together, and connecting together all those little matters which had preceded or followed some important event. She succeeded by sheer force of attention, by force of memory and of concentrated will power in bringing back to mind almost completely her two first years at Peuples. Distant memories of her life came back to her with a singular facility, bringing a kind of relief; but the later years seemed to lose themselves in a mist—to become mixt one with another: and sometimes she would stay for an indefinite time, her head bowed on one of the calendars, her mind full of the past, and yet not being able to remember whether it was in this or that calendar that such or such a remembrance ought to be tabulated. She placed them around the room like the pictures of the Way of the Cross—those tableaux of days that were no more. Then she would abruptly set down her chair before one of them; and there she would sit until night came, staring at it, immobile, buried in her dreams of remembrance.

One morning Rosalie came earlier than usual into her room, and said, setting down upon the table the bowl of coffee: "Come now, drink this up quickly. Denis is down-stairs waiting for us at the door. We are going over to Peuples to-day: I've got some business over there."

Jeanne thought that she was going to faint, so deep was her emotion. She drest herself, frightened and tremulous at the mere idea of seeing again that dear house.

A radiant sky spread out above over all the world, and the horse, in fits and starts of liveliness, sometimes broke into a gallop. When they entered into the commune of Etouvent, Jeanne's heart beat so fast that she could hardly breathe, and when she saw from a distance the brick pillars of the boundary-line of her old home, she exclaimed in a low voice two or three times, "Oh! —oh!—oh!—" as if something had happened to change her whole heart.

They left the wagon with the Couillards: then, while Rosalie and her son went off to attend to their business, the caretakers offered to take Jeanne over the château, the present owners of it being away; so they gave her the keys.

She set out alone, and when she was fairly before the old manor-house by the seaside, she stopt to look at it once again. It had changed in nothing outside. The large, grayish building that day showed upon its old walls the smile of the brilliant sunshine. All the shutters were closed.

A bit of a dead branch fell on her dress. She raised her eyes. It came from the plane-tree. She drew near the big tree with its smooth, pale bark; she stroked it with her hand as if it had been an animal. Her foot struck something in the grass—a fragment of rotten wood; it was the last fragment of the very bench on which she had sat so often with those of her own family about her; the very bench which had been seen set in place on the very day that Julien had made his first visit.

She reached the double doors of the vestibule of the house, and she had great trouble to open them; for the heavy, rusty key refused to turn in the lock. At length the lock yielded with a heavy grinding of its springs; and the door, a little obstinate itself, burst open with a cloud of dust.

At once, and almost running, she went upstairs to her own room. She could recognize it, hung as it was with a light new paper: but throwing open a window, she looked out and stood motionless, stirred even to the depth of her being at the sight of all that landscape, so much beloved; the shrubs, the elm-trees, the flat reaches, and the sea dotted with brown sails, motionless in the distance.

Then she began prowling about the great empty dwelling. She even stopt to look at the discolorations on the walls; spots familiar to her eyes. Once she stood before a little hole crusht in the plaster by the baron; who had often amused himself, when he was young, with making passages at arms, cane in hand, against the partition wall, when he happend to be passing this spot.

She went down-stairs to the drawing-room. It was somber behind the closed shutters: for some time she could not distinguish anything; then her eyes became accustomed to the darkness. Little by little she recognized the wide tapestries with their patterns of birds flitting about. Two settees were set before the chimney as if people had just quitted them; and the very odor of the room, an odor which it had always kept—that old, vague, sweet odor belonging to some old houses— entered Jeanne's very being, enwrapt her in souvenirs, intoxicated her memory. She remained gasping, breathing in that breath of the past, her eyes fixt upon those two chairs; for suddenly she saw—as she had so often seen them—her father and her mother, sitting there warming their feet by the fire. She started back terrified, struck her back against the edge of the door, caught at it to keep herself from falling, but kept her eyes still fixt upon the chairs.

The vision disappeared. For some moments she remained forgetful of everything; then slowly she recovered her self-possession, and would have fled from the room, fearful of losing her self-control. Her glance fell by chance on the door-post on which she was leaning; and there before her eyes were the marks that had been made to keep track of Poulet's height as he was growing up!

The little marks climbed the painted wood at irregular intervals; figures traced with the pen-knife noted down the different ages with the month of the boy's life. Sometimes the jottings were in the handwriting of the baron, a large hand; sometimes they were in her own smaller hand; sometimes in that of Aunt Lison, a little shaky. It seemed to her that the child of other days was actually there, before her, with his blond hair, pressing his little forehead against the wall so that his height could be measured. The baron was crying, "Jeanne! he has grown a whole centimeter in the last six weeks!" She began to kiss the piece of wood in a frenzy of love.

But some one was calling her from outside. It was Rosalie's voice: "Madame Jeanne, Madame Jeanne, we are waiting for you, to have luncheon." She went out in a trance. She hardly understood anything that the other said to her. She ate the things that they put on her plate; she listened without knowing what she heard, talking mechanically with the farming-women, who inquired about her health; she let them embrace her, and herself kissed the cheeks offered to her; and then got into the wagon again.

When she caught her last glimpse of the high roof of the château across the trees, she felt a terrible sinking in her heart. It seemed to her in her innermost being that she had said farewell forever to her old home!

GERMANY

1483—1859

MARTIN LUTHER

Born in 1483, died in 1546; his father a slate-cutter; studied at Magdeburg and Erfurt; against the wishes of his family, became a monk; went to Rome in 1510; published on the church door at Wittenburg in 1517 his thesis against the sale of indulgences; summoned to Rome, he refused to go and published further attacks upon the Church; excommunicated in 1520 and his writings publicly burned, whereupon he publicly burned the papal bull of excommunication; made his speech before the Diet of Worms in 1521; taken prisoner and confined in the Wartburg, he there translated the New Testament; later translated the Old Testament, and published a hymn-book; in 1525 married a nun; published numerous polemical pamphlets against the Church; had great influence in the formation of the present literary language of Germany.

SOME OF HIS TABLE TALK AND SAYINGS[1]

"BEFORE I translated the New Testament out of the Greek all longed after it; when it was done, their longing lasted scarce four weeks. Then they desired the books of Moses; when I had translated these, they had enough thereof in a short time. After that, they would have the Psalms; of these they were soon weary, and desired other books. So will it be with the Book of Ecclesiasticus, which they now long for, and about which I have taken great pains. All is

[1] Luther's "Table Talk" found English translators soon after it appeared in German. A notable later version was made by William Hazlitt.

79

acceptable until our giddy brains be satisfied; afterward we let things lie, and seek after new.''

Dr. Luther discust at length concerning witchcraft and charms. He said that his mother had had to undergo infinite annoyance from one of her neighbors, who was a witch and whom she was fain to conciliate with all sorts of attention, for this witch could throw a charm upon children which made them cry themselves to death. A pastor having punished her for some knavery, she cast a spell upon him by means of some earth upon which he had walked, and which she bewitched. The poor man hereupon fell sick of a malady which no remedy could remove, and shortly after died.

Dr. Luther said he had heard from the Elector of Saxony, John Frederic, that a powerful family in Germany was descended from the devil—the founder having been born of a succubus. He added this story: "A gentleman had a young and beautiful wife, who, dying, was buried. Shortly afterward, this gentleman and one of his servants sleeping in the same chamber, the wife who was dead came at night, bent over the bed of the gentleman as tho she were conversing with him, and after a while went away again. The servant, having twice observed this circumstance, asked his master whether he knew that every night a woman clothed in white stood by his bedside. The master replied that he had slept soundly, and had observed nothing of the sort. The next night he took care to remain awake. The woman came, and he asked her who she was and what she wanted. She answered that she was his wife. He returned, 'My wife is dead and buried.' She answered, she had died by reason of his sins; but that if he would receive her again, she would return to him in life. He said if it were possible, he should be well content. She told him he must undertake not to swear, as he was wont to do; for that if he ever did so, she should once more die, and permanently quit him. He promised this; and the dead woman, returning to seeming life, dwelt with him, ate, drank, and slept with him, and had children by him. One day that he had guests, his wife went to fetch some cakes from an adjoining apartment, and remained a long time absent. The gentleman grew impatient, and broke out into his old oaths. The wife not returning, the gentleman with his friends went to seek her, but she had disappeared; only the clothes she had worn lay on the floor. She was never again seen.''

"Between husband and wife there should be no question as to *meum* and *tuum*. All things should be in common between them, without any distinction or means of distinguishing."

"St. Augustine said finely: 'A marriage without children is the world without the sun.' ''

Dr. Luther said one day to his wife: "You make me do what you will; you have full sovereignty here, and I award you with all my heart the command in all household matters, reserving my rights in other points. Never any good came out of female domination. God created Adam master and lord of living creatures; but Eve spoilt all, when she persuaded him to set himself above God's will. 'Tis you women, with your tricks and artifices, that lead men into error."

" 'Tis a grand thing for a married pair to live

in perfect union, but the devil rarely permits
this. When they are apart, they can not endure
the separation; and when they are together, they
can not endure the always seeing one another.
'Tis as the poet says: '*Nec tecum vivere possum,
nec sine te.*' Married people must assiduously pray
against these assaults of the devil. I have seen
marriage where, at first, husband and wife
seemed as tho they would eat one another up;
in six months they have separated in mutual
disgust. 'Tis the devil inspires this evanescent
ardor, in order to divert the parties from
prayer."

Dr. Luther said, in reference to those who
write satirical attacks upon women, that such
will not go unpunished. "If the author be one
of high rank, rest assured he is not really of
noble origin, but a surreptitious intruder into the
family. What defects women have, we must check
them for in private, gently by word of mouth;
for woman is a frail vessel." The doctor then
turned round and said, "Let us talk of something
else."

There was at Frankfort-on-the-Oder a school-
master, a pious and learned man, whose heart was
fervently inclined to theology, and who had
preached several times with great applause. He
was called to the dignity of deacon; but his wife,
a violent, fierce woman, would not consent to
his accepting the charge, saying she would not
be the wife of a minister.

It became a question, what was the poor man
to do? which was he to renounce, his preacher-
ship or his wife? Luther at first said jocosely,
"Oh, if he has married, as you tell me, a widow,

he must needs obey her." But after a while he resumed severely: "The wife is bound to follow her husband, not the husband his wife. This must be an ill woman, nay, the devil incarnate, to be ashamed of a charge with which our Lord and his apostles were invested. If she were my wife, I should shortly say to her, 'Wilt thou follow me, aye or no? Reply forthwith'; and if she replied, 'No,' I would leave her, and take another wife."

I have no pleasure in any man who despises music. It is no invention of ours: it is the gift of God. I place it next to theology. Satan hates music: he knows how it drives the evil spirit out of us.

The strength and glory of a town does not depend on its wealth, its walls, its great mansions, its powerful armaments; but on the number of its learned, serious, kind, and well-educated citizens.

Greek and Latin are the scabbard which holds the sword of the Spirit, the cases which enclose the precious jewels, the vessels which contain the old wine, the baskets which carry the loaves and fishes for the feeding of the multitude.

Only a little of the first fruits of wisdom— only a few fragments of the boundless heights, breadths, and depths of truth—have I been able to gather.

My own writings are like a wild forest, compared with the gentle, limpid fluency of his [Brenz's] language. If small things dare be compared with great, my words are like the Spirit of Elijah—a great and strong wind, rending the mountains and breaking in pieces the rocks; and his is the still small voice. But yet God uses also coarse wedges for splitting coarse blocks; and besides the fructifying grain, he employs also the rending thunder and lightning to purify the atmosphere.

I must root out the stumps and trunks, and I am a rough woodsman who must break the road and prepare it: but Magister Philip [Melanchthon] goes on quietly and gently, plows and plants, sows and waters joyfully.

Be temperate with your children; punish them if they lie or steal, but be just in what you do. It is a lighter sin to take pears and apples than to take money. I shudder when I think what I went through myself. My mother beat me about some nuts once till the blood came. I had a terrible time of it; but she meant well.

Never be hard with children. Many a fine character has been ruined by the stupid brutality of pedagogs. The parts of speech are a boy's pillory. I was myself flogged fifteen times in one forenoon, over the conjugation of a verb. Punish if you must; but be kind too, and let the sugar-plum go with the rod.

My being such a small creature was a misfortune for the Pope. He despised me too much. What, he thought, could a slave like me do to him—to him who was the greatest man in the world? Had he accepted my proposal he would have extinguished me.

The better a man is, the more clearly he sees how little he is good for, and the greater mockery it is to him to hold the notion that he has deserved reward. Miserable creatures that we are, we earn our bread in sin. Till we are seven years old, we do nothing but eat and drink and sleep and play; from seven to twenty-one we study four hours a day, the rest of it we run about and amuse ourselves; then we work till fifty, and then we grow again to be children. We sleep half our lives; we give God a tenth of our time; and yet we think that with our good works we can merit heaven. What have I been doing to-day? I have talked for two hours, I have been at meals three hours, I have been idle four hours; ah, enter not into judgment with thy servant, O Lord!

The principle of marriage runs through all creation, and flowers as well as animals are male and female.

If a man could make a single rose, we should give him an empire; yet roses, and flowers no less beautiful, are scattered in profusion over the world, and no one regards them.

GOTTHOLD EPHRAIM LESSING

Born in 1729, died in 1781; studied theology at Leipsic, but turned his thoughts to writing for the stage, his first comedy being produced in 1748; settled in Berlin in 1748; lived in Leipsic a second time, engaged in writing plays, poems and books; removed from Berlin to Breslau in 1765, where he wrote his masterpiece, "Laocoön," published in 1766; in 1769 made librarian of the ducal library in Wolfenbüttel, which place he held until his death.

I

POETRY AND PAINTING COMPARED[1]

THE first person who compared painting and poetry with one another was a man of refined feeling, who became aware of a similar effect produced upon himself by both arts. He felt both represent what is absent as if it were present, and appearance as if it were reality; that both deceived, and that the deception of both is pleasing.

A second observer sought to penetrate below the surface of this pleasure, and discovered that in both it flowed from the same source. Beauty, the idea of which we first deduce from bodily

[1] From the preface to the "Laocoön." Translated by E. C. Beasley and Helen Zimmern. An earlier translation of the "Laocoön" was made by William Ross in 1836.

objects, possesses universal laws, applicable to more things than one; to actions and to thoughts as well as to forms.

A third reflected upon the value and distribution of these universal laws, and noticed that some are more predominant in painting, others in poetry; that thus, in the latter case, poetry will help to explain and illustrate painting; in the former, painting will do the same for poetry.

The first was the amateur, the second the philosopher, the third the critic.

The first two could not easily make a wrong use of either their feelings or conclusions. On the other hand, the value of the critic's observations mainly depends upon the correctness of their application to the individual case; and since for one clear-sighted critic there have always been fifty ingenious ones, it would have been a wonder if this application had always been applied with all that caution which is required to hold the balance equally between the two arts.

If Apelles and Protogenes, in their lost writings on painting, affirmed and illustrated its laws by the previously established rules of poetry, we may feel sure that they did it with that moderation and accuracy with which we now see, in the works of Aristotle, Cicero, Horace, and Quintilian, the principles and experience of painting applied to eloquence and poetry. It is the privilege of the ancients never in any matter to do too much or too little.

But in many points we moderns have imagined that we have advanced far beyond them, because we have changed their narrow lanes into highways, even tho the shorter and safer highways contract into footpaths as they lead through deserts.

The dazzling antithesis of the Greek Voltaire, "Painting is dumb poetry, and poetry is speaking painting," can never have been found in any didactic work; it was an idea, amongst others, of Simonides, and the truth it contains is so evident that we feel compelled to overlook the indistinctness and error which accompany it.

And yet the ancients did not overlook them. They confined the expression of Simonides to the effect of either art, but at the same time forgot not to inculcate that, notwithstanding the complete similarity of this effect, the two were different, both in the objects which they imitated, and in their mode of imitation.

But, just as tho no such difference existed, many recent critics have drawn from this harmony of poetry and painting the most ill-digested conclusions. At one time they compress poetry into the narrower limits of painting; at another they allow painting to occupy the whole wide sphere of poetry. Everything, say they, that the one is entitled to should be conceded to the other; everything that pleases or displeases in the one is necessarily pleasing or displeasing in the other. Full of this idea, they give utterance in the most confident tone to the most shallow decisions; when, criticizing the works of a poet and painter upon the same subject, they set down as faults any divergences they may observe, laying the blame upon the one or the other accordingly as they may have more taste for poetry or for painting.

Indeed, this false criticism has misled in some

degree the professors of art. It has produced the love of description in poetry, and of allegory in painting: while the critics strove to reduce poetry to a speaking painting, without properly knowing what it could and ought to paint; and painting to a dumb poem, without having considered in what degree it could express general ideas without alienating itself from its destiny, and degenerating into an arbitrary method of writing.

II

OF SUFFERING HELD IN RESTRAINT [2]

HERR WINCKELMANN has pronounced a noble simplicity and quiet grandeur, displayed in the posture no less than in the expression, to be the characteristic features common to all the Greek masterpieces of painting and sculpture. "As," says he, "the depths of the sea always remain calm, however much the surface may be raging, so the expression in the figures of the Greeks, under every form of passion, shows a great and self-collected soul.

"This spirit is portrayed in the countenance of Laocoön, and not in the countenance alone, under the most violent suffering; the pain discovers itself in every muscle and sinew of his body, and the beholder, while looking at the agonized contraction of the abdomen, without

[2] From Chapter I of the "Laocoön." Translated by E. C. Beasley and Helen Zimmern.

viewing the face and the other parts, believes that he almost feels the pain himself. This pain expresses itself, however, without any violence, both in the features and in the whole posture. He raises no terrible shriek, such as Virgil makes his Laocoön utter, for the opening of the mouth does not admit it; it is rather an anxious and supprest sigh, as described by Sadoleto. The pain of body and grandeur of soul are, as it were, weighed out, and distributed with equal strength through the whole frame of the figure. Laocoön suffers, but he suffers as the Philoctetes of Sophocles; his misery pierces us to the very soul, but inspires us with a wish that we could endure misery like that great man.

"The expressing of so great a soul is far higher than the painting of beautiful nature. The artist must have felt within himself that strength of spirit which he imprinted upon his marble. Greece had philosophers and artists in one person, and more than one Metrodorus. Philosophy gave her hand to art, and breathed into its figures more than ordinary souls."

The observation on which the foregoing remarks are founded, "that the pain in the face of Laocoön does not show itself with that force which its intensity would have led us to expect," is perfectly correct. Moreover, it is indisputable that it is in this very point where the half-connoisseur would have decided that the artist had fallen short of nature, and had not reached the true pathos of pain, that his wisdom is particularly conspicuous.

But I confess I differ from Winckelmann as to what is in his opinion the basis of this wisdom, and as to the universality of the rule which he deduces from it.

I acknowledge that I was startled, first by the glance of disapproval which he casts upon Virgil, and secondly by the comparison with Philoctetes. From this point then I shall set out, and write down my thoughts as they were developed in me.

"Laocoön suffers as Sophocles' Philoctetes." But how does the latter suffer? It is curious that his sufferings should leave such a different impression behind them. The cries, the shrieking, the wild imprecations, with which he filled the camp, and interrupted all the sacrifices and holy rites, resound no less horribly through his desert island, and were the cause of his being banished to it. The same sounds of despondency, sorrow, and despair fill the theater in the poet's imitation. It has been observed that the third act of this piece is shorter than the others; from this it may be gathered, say the critics, that the ancients took little pains to preserve a uniformity of length in the different acts. I quite agree with them, but I should rather ground my opinion upon another example than this. The sorrowful exclamations and the moanings, of which this act consists, must have been pronounced with tensions and breakings off altogether different from those required in a continuous speech, and doubtless made this act last quite as long in the representation as the others. It appears much shorter to the reader, when seen on paper, than it must have done to the audience in a theater.

A cry is the natural expression of bodily pain. Homer's wounded heroes frequently fall with cries to the ground. He makes Venus, when

merely scratched, shriek aloud; not that he may
thereby paint the effeminacy of the goddess of
pleasure, but rather that he may give suffering
Nature her due; for even the iron Mars, when
he feels the lance of Diomedes, shrieks so horribly that his cries are like those of ten thousand
furious warriors, and fill both armies with horror.
Tho Homer, in other respects, raises his heroes
above human nature, they always remain faithful
to it in matters connected with the feeling of
pain and insult, or its expression through cries,
tears, or reproaches. In their actions they are
beings of a higher order, in their feelings true
men.

I know that we, more refined Europeans, of
a wiser and later age, know how to keep our
mouths and eyes under closer restraint. We are
forbidden by courtesy and propriety to cry and
weep; and with us the active bravery of the first
rough age of the world has been changed into
a passive. Yet even our own ancestors, tho barbarians, were greater in the latter than in the
former. To suppress all pain, to meet the stroke
of death with unflinching eye, to die laughing
under the bites of adders, to lament neither their
sins nor the loss of their dearest friends—these
were the characteristics of the old heroic courage
of the north. Palnatoki forbade his Jomsburgers
either to fear or so much as to mention the name
of fear.

Not so the Greek. He felt and feared. He
gave utterance to his pain and sorrow. He was
ashamed of no human weaknesses, only none of
them must hold him back from the path of honor,
or impede him in the fulfilment of his duty.

What in the barbarian sprang from habit and ferocity arose from principle in the Greek. With him heroism was as the spark concealed in flint, which, so long as no external force awakens it, sleeps in quiet, nor robs the stone either of its clearness or its coldness. With the barbarian it was a bright consuming flame, which was ever roaring, and devoured, or at least blackened, every other good quality. Thus, when Homer makes the Trojans march to the combat with wild cries, the Greeks, on the contrary, in resolute silence, the critics justly observe that the poet intended to depict the one as barbarians, the other as a civilized people. I wonder that they have not remarked a similar contrast of character in another passage. The hostile armies have made a truce; they are busied with burning their dead; and these rites are accompanied on both sides with the warm flow of tears. But Priam forbids the Trojans to weep. He forbade them to weep, says Dacier, because he feared the effect would be too softening, and that on the morrow they would go with less courage to the battle. True! But why, I ask, should Priam only fear this result? Why does not Agamemnon also lay the same prohibition on the Greeks? The poet has a deeper meaning; he wishes to teach us that the civilized Greek could be brave at the same time that he wept, while in the uncivilized Trojan all human feelings were to be previously stifled.

It is worth observing that among the few tragedies which have come down to us from antiquity two are found in which bodily pain constitutes not the lightest part of the misfortune which befalls the suffering heroes—the Philoctetes and the dying Hercules. Sophocles paints the last also as moaning and shrieking, weeping and crying. Thanks to our polite neighbors, those masters of propriety, no such ridiculous and intolerable characters as a moaning Philoctetes or a shrieking Hercules will ever again appear upon the stage. One of their latest poets has indeed ventured upon a Philoctetes, but would he have dared to exhibit the true one?

Even a Laocoön is found among the lost plays of Sophocles. Would that fate had spared it to us! The slight mention which some old grammarians have made of it affords us no ground for concluding how the poet had handled his subject; but of this I feel certain, that Laocoön would not have been drawn more stoically than Philoctetes and Hercules. All stoicism is undramatical; and our sympathy is always proportioned to the suffering exprest by the object which interests us. It is true if we see him bear his misery with a great soul, this grandeur of soul excites our admiration; but admiration is only a cold emotion, and its inactive astonishment excludes every warmer passion as well as every distinct idea.

I now come to my inference; if it be true that a cry at the sensation of bodily pain, particularly according to the old Greek way of thinking, is quite compatible with greatness of soul, it can not have been for the sake of expressing such greatness that the artist avoided imitating this shriek in marble. Another reason therefore must be found for his here deviating from his rival, the poet, who expresses it with the highest purpose.

JOHANN WOLFGANG VON GOETHE

Born in Frankfurt in 1749, died in Weimar in 1832; the greatest name in German literature; his father an imperial councilor; studied jurisprudence at Leipsic; settled in Weimar in 1775, where he became privy councilor, and in 1782 was ennobled and made President of the Ducal Chamber; traveled in Italy in 1786-88; served in the war against France in 1792-93; began his friendship with Schiller in 1794; published "The Sorrows of Werther" in 1774, "Hermann and Dorothea" in 1797, "Faust" first part, in 1808, his "Italian Journey" in 1817, "Wilhelm Meister," the several parts in 1778, 1796, 1821, and 1829; the second part of "Faust" in 1831.

I

ON FIRST READING SHAKESPEARE [1]

"HAVE you never," said Jarno, taking him aside, "read one of Shakespeare's plays?"

"No," replied Wilhelm: "since the time when they became more known in Germany, I have myself grown unacquainted with the theater; and know not whether I should now rejoice that an old taste and occupation of my youth has been by chance renewed. In the meantime, all that I have heard of these plays has excited little wish to become acquainted with such extraor-

[1] From "Wilhelm Meister." Translated by Thomas Carlyle. This translation by Carlyle was published in Edinburgh in 1824 and was contemporary with Carlyle's translation of "Legendre" and his "Life of Schiller."

dinary monsters, which appear to set probability and dignity alike at defiance.''

"I would advise you,'' said the other, "to make a trial, notwithstanding: it can do one no harm to look at what is extraordinary with one's own eyes. I will lend you a volume or two; and you can not better spend your time than by casting everything aside, and retiring to the solitude of your old habitation, to look into the magic lantern of that unknown world. It is sinful of you to waste your hours in dressing out these apes to look more human, and teaching dogs to dance. One thing only I require—you must not cavil at the form; the rest I can leave to your own good sense and feeling.''

The horses were standing at the door; and Jarno mounted with some other cavaliers to go and hunt. Wilhelm looked after him with sadness. He would fain have spoken much with this man who tho in a harsh, unfriendly way, gave him new ideas—ideas that he had need of.

Oftentimes a man, when approaching some development of his powers, capacities, and conceptions, gets into a perplexity from which a prudent friend might easily deliver him. He resembles a traveler, who, at but a short distance from the inn he is to rest at, falls into the water: were any one to catch him then and pull him to the bank, with one good wetting it were over; whereas, tho he struggles out himself, it is often at the side where he tumbled in, and he has to make a wide and weary circuit before reaching his appointed object.

Wilhelm now began to have an inkling that things went forward in the world differently from

what he had supposed. He now viewed close at
hand the solemn and imposing life of the great
and distinguished, and wondered at the easy dignity which they contrived to give it. An army
on its march, a princely hero at the head of it,
such a multitude of cooperating warriors, such
a multitude of crowding worshipers, exalted his
imagination. In this mood he received the promised books; and ere long, as may be easily supposed, the stream of that mighty genius laid hold
of him and led him down to a shoreless ocean,
where he soon completely forgot and lost himself. . . .

Wilhelm had scarcely read one or two of Shakespeare's plays till their effect on him became so
strong that he could go no further. His whole
soul was in commotion. He sought an opportunity to speak with Jarno; to whom, on meeting
with him, he exprest his boundless gratitude for
such delicious entertainment.

"I clearly enough foresaw," said Jarno, "that
you would not remain insensible to the charms
of the most extraordinary and most admirable of
all writers."

"Yes!" exclaimed our friend: "I can not recollect that any book, any man, any incident of
my life, has produced such important effects on
me as the precious works to which by your kindness I have been directed. They seem as if they
were performances of some celestial genius de-
scending among men, to make them by the mildest
instructions acquainted with themselves. They
are no fictions! You would think, while reading
them, you stood before the enclosed awful Books
of Fate, while the whirlwind of most impassioned

life was howling through the leaves, and tossing them fiercely to and fro. The strength and tenderness, the power and peacefulness of this man have so astonished and transported me that I long vehemently for the time when I shall have it in my power to read further."

"Bravo!" said Jarno, holding out his hand, and squeezing our friend's. "This is as it should be! And the consequences which I hope for will likewise surely follow."

"I wish," said Wilhelm, "I could but disclose to you all that is going on within me even now. All the anticipations I have ever had regarding man and his destiny, which have accompanied me from youth upward often unobserved by myself, I find developed and fulfilled in Shakespeare's writings. It seems as if he cleared up every one of our enigmas to us, tho we can not say, Here or there is the word of solution. His men appear like natural men, and yet they are not. These, the most mysterious and complex productions of creation, here act before us as if they were watches, whose dial-plates and cases were of crystal, which pointed out according to their use their course of the hours and minutes; while at the same time you could discern the combination of wheels and springs that turn them. The few glances I have cast over Shakespeare's world incite me, more than anything beside, to quicken my footsteps forward into the actual world, to mingle in the flood of destinies that is suspended over it; and at length, if I shall prosper, to draw a few cups from the great ocean of true nature, and to distribute them from off the stage among the thirsting people of my native land."

II

THE CORONATION OF JOSEPH II [2]

THE coronation-day dawned at last, on the 3d of April, 1764; the weather was favorable, and everybody was in motion. I, with several of my relations and friends, had been provided with a good place in one of the upper stories of the Römer itself, where we might completely survey the whole. We betook ourselves to the spot very early in the morning, and from above, as in a bird's-eye view, contemplated the arrangements which we had inspected more closely the day before. There was the newly-erected fountain, with two large tubs on the left and right, into which the double-eagle on the post was to pour from its two beaks white wine on this side and red wine on that. There, gathered into a heap, lay the oats; here stood the large wooden hut, in which we had several days since seen the whole fat ox roasted and basted on a huge spit before a charcoal fire. All the avenues leading out from the Römer, and from other streets back to the Römer, were secured on both sides by barriers and guards. The great square was gradually

[2] From the Twelfth Book of the "Autobiography: Truth and Poetry from My Own Life." Translated by John Oxenford. A year before the date of Oxenford's translation (1848) Parke Godwin of New York had published a translation. Joseph II was the son of Francis I and Maria Theresa and was crowned King of the Romans (that is, of the Holy Roman Empire) in 1764 and succeeded to the German Empire in 1765.

filled, and the waving and pressure grew every moment stronger and more in motion, as the multitude always, if possible, endeavored to reach the spot where some new scene arose, and something particular was announced.

All this time there reigned a tolerable stillness, and when the alarm-bells were sounded, all the people seemed struck with terror and amazement. What first attracted the attention of all who could overlook the square from above was the train in which the lords of Aix and Nuremberg brought the crown-jewels to the cathedral. These, as palladia, had been assigned the first place in the carriage, and the deputies sat before them on the back seat with becoming reverence. Now the three electors betake themselves to the cathedral. After the presentation of the insignia to the Elector of Mentz, the crown and sword are immediately carried to the imperial quarters. The further arrangements and manifold ceremonies occupied, in the interim, the chief persons, as well as the spectators, in the church, as we other well-informed persons could well imagine.

In the meanwhile before our eyes the ambassadors ascended to the Römer, from which the canopy is carried by the under-officers into the imperial quarters. The Hereditary Marshal, Count von Pappenheim, instantly mounts his horse; he was a very handsome slender gentleman, whom the Spanish costume, the rich doublet, the gold mantle, the high feathered hat, and the loose flying hair, became very well. He puts himself in motion, and amid the sound of all the bells, the ambassadors follow him on horseback to the quarters of the Emperor in still greater

magnificence than on the day of election. One
would have liked to be there too, as indeed on
this day it would have been altogether desirable
to multiply one's self. However, we told each
other what was going on there. Now the Emperor is putting on his domestic robes, we said
a new dress, and after the old Carolingian pattern. The hereditary officers receive the insignia,
and with them get on horseback. The Emperor
in his robes, the Roman King in the Spanish
habit, immediately mount their steeds; and while
this is done, the endless procession which precedes
them has already announced them.

The eye was already wearied by the multitude
of richly-drest attendants and magistrates, and
by the nobility who, in stately fashion, were
moving along; but when the electoral envoys, the
hereditary officers, and at last, under the richly-
embroidered canopy, borne by twelve Schöffen
and senators, the Emperor, in romantic costume,
and to the left, a little behind him, in the Spanish
dress, his son, slowly floated along on magnificently adorned horses, the eye was no more
sufficient for the sight. One would have liked
to detain the scene, but for a moment, by a magic
charm; but the glory passed on without stopping,
and the space that was scarcely quitted was
immediately filled again by the crowd, which
poured in like billows.

But now a new pressure took place; for another
approach from the market to the Römer gate had
to be opened, and a road of planks to be bridged
over it, on which the train returning from the
cathedral was to walk.

What passed within the cathedral, the endless

ceremonies which precede and accompany the anointing, the crowning, the dubbing of knighthood—all this we were glad to hear told afterward by those who had sacrificed much else to be present in the church.

The rest of us, in the interim, partook of a frugal repast; for in this festal day we had to be contented with cold meat. But, on the other hand, the best and oldest wine had been brought out of all the family-cellars, so that in this respect at least we celebrated the ancient festival in ancient style.

In the square the sight most worth seeing was now the bridge, which had been finished and covered with orange and white cloth; and we who had stared at the Emperor, first in his carriage and then on horseback, were now to admire him walking on foot. Singularly enough, the last pleased us the most; for we thought that in this way he exhibited himself both in the most natural and in the most dignified manner.

Older persons, who were present at the coronation of Francis the First, related that Maria Theresa, beautiful beyond measure, had looked on this solemnity from a balcony window of the Frauenstein house, close to the Römer. As her consort returned from the cathedral in his strange costume, and seemed to her, so to speak, like a ghost of Charlemagne, he had, as if in jest, raised both his hands, and shown her the imperial globe, the scepter, and the curious gloves, at which she had broken out into immoderate laughter, which served for the great delight and edification of the crowd, which was thus honored with a sight of the good and natural matrimonial understanding between the most exalted couple of Christendom. But when the Empress, to greet her consort, waved her handkerchief, and even shouted a loud vivat to him, the enthusiasm and exultation of the people was raised to the highest, so that there was no end to the cheers of joy. . . .

The rejoicings, which resounded from the market-place, now spread likewise over the great square, and a boisterous vivat burst forth from thousands upon thousands of throats, and doubtless from as many hearts. For this grand festival was to be the pledge of a lasting peace, which indeed for many a long year actually blest Germany.

Several days before it had been made known by public proclamation that neither the bridge nor the eagle over the fountain were to be exposed to the people, and were therefore not, as at other times, to be touched. This was done to prevent the mischief inevitable with such a rush of persons. But in order to sacrifice in some degree to the genius of the mob persons expressly appointed went behind the procession, loosened the cloth from the bridge, wound it up like a flag, and threw it into the air. This gave rise to no disaster, but to a laughable mishap; for the cloth unrolled itself in the air, and, as it fell, covered a larger or smaller number of persons. Those now who took hold of the ends and drew them toward themselves, pulled all those in the middle to the ground, enveloped them and teased them till they tore or cut themselves through, and everybody, in his own way, had borne off a corner of the stuff made sacred by the footsteps of majesty. . . .

It was precisely at the right time that I again took possession of my window; for the most remarkable part of all that was to be seen in public was just about to take place. All the people had turned toward the Römer, and a re-iterated shout of vivat gave us to understand that the Emperor and King in their vestments were showing themselves to the populace from the balcony of the great hall. But they were not alone to serve as a spectacle, since another strange spectacle occurred before their eyes. First of all, the handsome slender Hereditary Marshal flung himself upon his steed; he had laid aside his sword; in his right hand he held a silver-handled vessel, and a tin spatula in his left. He rode within the barriers to the great heap of oats, sprang in, filled the vessel to overflow, smoothed it off, and carried it back again with great dignity. The imperial stable was now provided for. The Hereditary Chamberlain then rode likewise to the spot, and brought back a basin with ewer and towel. But more entertaining for the spectators was the Hereditary Carver, who came to fetch a piece of the roasted ox. He also rode, with a silver dish, through the barriers, to the large wooden kitchen, and came forth again with his portion covered, that he might go back to the Römer. Now it was the turn of the Hereditary Cupbearer, who rode to the fountain and fetched wine. Thus now was the imperial table furnished, and every eye waited upon the Hereditary Treasurer, who was to throw about the money. . . .

Everybody knew now that the Emperor and King would return from the cabinet whither

they had retired from the balcony, and feast in
the great hall of the Römer. We had been able
to admire the arrangements made for it the day
before; and my most anxious wish was, if possible, to look in to-day. I repaired, therefore,
by the usual path, to the great staircase, which
stands directly opposite the door of the hall.
Here I gazed at the distinguished personages who
this day acted as the servants of the head of
the empire. Forty-four counts, all splendidly
drest, passed me, carrying the dishes from the
kitchen, so that the contrast between their dignity and their occupation might well be bewil-
dering to a boy. The crowd was not great, but
considering the little space, sufficiently percep-
tible. The hall-door was guarded, while those
who were authorized went frequently in and out.
I saw one of the Palatine domestic officials, whom
I asked whether he could not take me in with
him. He did not deliberate long, but gave me
one of the silver vessels he just then bore—which
he could do so much the more as I was neatly
clad; and thus I reached the sanctuary. The
Palatine buffet stood to the left, directly by the
door, and with some steps I placed myself on
the elevation of it, behind the barriers.

At the other end of the hall, immediately by
the windows, raised on the steps of the throne,
and under canopies, sat the Emperor and King
in their robes; but the crown and scepter lay
some distance behind them on gold cushions. The
three spiritual electors, their buffets behind them,
had taken their places on single elevations; the
Elector of Mentz opposite their majesties, the
Elector of Treves at the right, and the Elector of

Cologne at the left. This upper part of the hall was imposing and cheerful to behold, and excited the remark that the spiritual power likes to keep as long as possible with the ruler. On the contrary, the buffets and tables of all the temporal electors, which were, indeed, magnificently ornamented, but without occupants, made one think of the misunderstanding which had gradually arisen for centuries between them and the head of the empire. Their ambassadors had already withdrawn to eat in a side-chamber; and if the greater part of the hall assumed a sort of spectral appearance, by so many invisible guests being so magnificently attended, a large unfurnished table in the middle was still more sad to look upon; for there also many covers stood empty, because all those who had certainly a right to sit there had, for appearance sake, kept away, that on the greatest day of honor they might not renounce any of their honor, if indeed they were then to be found in the city.

FRIEDRICH VON SCHILLER

Born in 1759, died in 1808; his father a lieutenant in the
Seven Years' War; published "The Robbers" in 1781, printing it at his own expense; incurred the displeasure of the
Duke of Wurtenberg and removed to Bauerback near Meinin-
gen, where he lived until 1783 under the name of Dr.
Schmidt; published "Love and Intrigue" in 1784; removed
to Leipsic in 1785, and thence to Dresden; published
"Don Carlos" in 1787; removed to Weimar in 1787;
published "Revolt of the Netherlands" in 1788; professor of history at Jena in 1789; published "History
of the Thirty Years' War" in 1790-93; began his
friendship with Goethe in 1794; published "Wallenstein's
Camp" in 1799; followed by "Piccolomini," "Wallenstein's
Death," "Marie Stuart" (1801), "The Maid of Orleans"
(1802); ennobled by the Emperor in 1802; published "William Tell" in 1804.

I

THE BATTLE OF LUTZEN [1]
(1632)

At last the fateful morning dawned; but an
impenetrable fog which spread over the plain
delayed the attack till noon. Kneeling in front
of his lines, the King offered up his devotions;
and the whole army, at the same moment drop-

[1] From the "History of the Thirty Years' War." Translated
by A. J. W. Morrison. Schiller's work had already been translated by Captain Blaqurelle in 1799 and by J. M. Duncan in
1828. Another version is by G. Moir. The battle of Lutzen was
fought between Swedes, numbering 18,000, led by Gustavus
Adolphus, and Imperialists, numbering about 30,000, under
Wallenstein. Gustavus Adolphus was killed in this battle.
On the same field in 1813, Napoleon defeated the combined
armies of Russia and Prussia.

ping on their knees, burst into a moving hymn, accompanied by the military music. The King then mounted his horse, and, clad only in a leather doublet and surtout (for a wound he had formerly received prevented his wearing armor), rode along the ranks, to animate the courage of his troops with a joyful confidence, which, however, the foreboding presentiment of his own bosom contradicted. "God with us!" was the war-cry of the Swedes; "Jesus Maria!" that of the Imperialists. About eleven the fog began to disperse, and the enemy became visible. At the same moment Lutzen was seen in flames, having been set on fire by command of the duke, to prevent his being outflanked on that side. The charge was now sounded; the cavalry rushed upon the enemy, and the infantry advanced against the trenches.

Received by a tremendous fire of musketry and heavy artillery, these intrepid battalions maintained the attack with undaunted courage, till the enemy's musketeers abandoned their posts, the trenches were passed, the battery carried and turned against the enemy. They prest forward with irresistible impetuosity; the first of the five Imperial brigades was immediately routed, the second soon after, and the third put to flight. But here the genius of Wallenstein opposed itself to their progress. With the rapidity of lightning he was on the spot to rally his discomfited troops; and his powerful word was sufficient to stop the flight of the fugitives. Supported by three regiments of cavalry, the vanquished brigades, forming anew, faced the enemy, and prest vigorously into the broken ranks of the Swedes. A murderous conflict ensued. The nearness of the enemy left no room for firearms, the fury of the attack no time for loading; man was matched to man, the useless musket exchanged for the sword and pike, and science gave way to desperation. Overpowered by numbers, the wearied Swedes at last retire beyond the trenches, and the captured battery is again lost by the retreat. A thousand mangled bodies already strewed the plain, and as yet not a single step of ground had been won.

In the mean time the King's right wing, led by himself, had fallen upon the enemy's left. The first impetuous shock of the heavy Finland cuirassiers dispersed the lightly-mounted Poles and Croats who were posted here, and their disorderly flight spread terror and confusion among the rest of the cavalry. At this moment notice was brought the King that his infantry were retreating over the trenches, and also that his left wing, exposed to a severe fire from the enemy's cannon posted at the windmills, was beginning to give way. With rapid decision he committed to General Horn the pursuit of the enemy's left, while he flew, at the head of the regiment of Steinbock, to repair the disorder of his right wing. His noble charger bore him with the velocity of lightning across the trenches, but the squadrons that followed could not come on with the same speed, and only a few horsemen, among whom was Francis Albert, Duke of Saxe-Lauenburg, were able to keep up with the King. He rode directly to the place where his infantry were most closely prest, and while he was reconnoitering the enemy's line for an exposed point of attack, the shortness of his sight unfortunately led him too close to their ranks.

An imperial Gefreiter remarking that every one respectfully made way for him as he rode along, immediately ordered a musketeer to take aim at him. "Fire at him yonder," said he: "that must be a man of consequence." The soldier fired, and the King's left arm was shattered. At that moment his squadron came hurrying up, and a confused cry of "The King bleeds! the King is shot!" spread terror and consternation through all the ranks. "It is nothing! follow me," cried the King, collecting his whole strength; but, overcome by pain, and nearly fainting, he requested the Duke of Lauenburg, in French to lead him unobserved out of the tumult. While the duke proceeded toward the right wing with the King, making a long circuit to keep this discouraging sight from the disordered infantry, his Majesty received a second shot through the back which deprived him of his remaining strength. "Brother," said he, with a dying voice, "I have enough! look only to your own life." At the same moment he fell from his horse, pierced by several more shots; and, abandoned by all his attendants, he breathed his last amidst the plundering bands of the Croats. His charger, flying without its rider, and covered with blood, soon made known to the Swedish cavalry the fall of their King. They rushed madly forward to rescue his sacred remains from the hands of the enemy. A murderous conflict ensued over the body, till his mangled remains were buried beneath a heap of slain.

The mournful tidings soon ran through the

Swedish army; but, instead of destroying the courage of these brave troops, it but excited it into a new, a wild and consuming flame. Life had lessened in value, now that the most sacred life of all was gone; death had no terrors for the lowly since the anointed head was not spared. With the fury of lions the Upland, Smaland, Finland, East and West Gothland regiments rushed a second time upon the left wing of the enemy, which, already making but feeble resistance to General Horn, was now entirely beaten from the field. Bernard, Duke of Saxe-Weimar, gave to the bereaved Swedes a noble leader in his own person; and the spirit of Gustavus led his victorious squadrons anew. The left wing quickly formed again and vigorously prest the right of the Imperialists. The artillery at the windmills, which had maintained so murderous a fire upon the Swedes, was captured and turned against the enemy. The center, also, of the Swedish infantry, commanded by the duke and Knyphausen, advanced a second time against the trenches, which they successfully passed, and retook the battery of seven cannons. The attack was now renewed with redoubled fury upon the heavy battalions of the enemy's center; their resistance became gradually less, and chance conspired with Swedish valor to complete the defeat. The imperial powder-wagons took fire, and, with a tremendous explosion, grenades and bombs filled the air. The enemy, now in confusion, thought they were attacked in the rear, while the Swedish brigades prest them in front. Their courage began to fail them. Their left wing was already beaten, their right wavering, and their artillery in the enemy's hands. The battle seemed to be almost decided; another moment would decide the fate of the day, when Pappenheim appeared on the field, with his cuirassiers and dragoons: all the advantages already gained were lost, and the battle was to be fought anew.

The order which recalled that general to Lutzen had reached him in Halle, while his troops were still plundering that town. It was impossible to collect the scattered infantry with that rapidity which the urgency of the order and Pappenheim's impatience required. Without waiting for it, therefore, he ordered eight regiments of cavalry to mount, and at their head he galloped at full speed for Lutzen, to share in the battle. He arrived in time to witness the flight of the Imperial right wing, which Gustavus Horn was driving from the field, and to be at first involved in their rout. But with rapid presence of mind he rallied the flying troops, and led them once more against the enemy. Carried away by his wild bravery, and impatient to encounter the King, who he supposed was at the head of this wing, he burst furiously upon the Swedish ranks, which, exhausted by victory and inferior in numbers were after a noble resistance, overpowered by this fresh body of enemies. Pappenheim's unexpected appearance revived the drooping courage of the Imperialists, and the Duke of Friedland quickly availed himself of the favorable moment to reform his line.

The closely-serried battalions of the Swedes were, after a tremendous conflict, again driven across the trenches, and the battery, which had been twice lost, again rescued from their hands.

The whole yellow regiment, the finest of all that distinguished themselves in this dreadful day, lay dead on the field, covering the ground almost in the same excellent order which, when alive, they maintained with such unyielding courage. The same fate befell another regiment of Blues, which Count Piccolomini attacked with the imperial cavalry and cut down after a desperate contest. Seven times did this intrepid general renew the attack; seven horses were shot under him, and he himself was pierced with six musket-balls; yet he would not leave the field until he was carried along in the general rout of the whole army. Wallenstein himself was seen riding through his ranks with cool intrepidity, amidst a shower of balls, assisting the distrest, encouraging the valiant with praise and the wavering by his fearful glance. Around and close by him his men were falling thick, and his own mantle was perforated by several shots. But avenging destiny this day protected that breast for which another weapon was reserved; on the same field where the noble Gustavus expired, Wallenstein was not allowed to terminate his guilty career.

Less fortunate was Pappenheim, the Telamon of the army, the bravest soldier of Austria and the Church. An ardent desire to encounter the King in person carried this daring leader into the thickest of the fight, where he thought his noble opponent was most surely to be met. Gustavus had also exprest a wish to meet his brave antagonist, but these hostile wishes remained ungratified; death first brought together these two great heroes. Two musket-balls pierced the breast of Pappenheim, and his men forcibly carried him from the field. While they were conveying him to the rear, a murmur reached him that he whom he had sought lay dead upon the plain. When the truth of the report was confirmed to him, his look became brighter, his dying eye sparkled with a last gleam of joy. "Tell the Duke of Friedland," said he, "that I lie without hope of life, but that I die happy, since I know that the implacable enemy of my religion has fallen on the same day."

With Pappenheim the good fortune of the Imperialists departed. The cavalry of the left wing, already beaten, and only rallied by his exertions, no sooner missed their victorious leader than they gave up everything for lost and abandoned the field of battle in spiritless despair. The right field fell into the same confusion, with the exception of a few regiments which the bravery of their colonels, Gotz, Terzky, Colloredo, and Piccolomini, compelled to keep their ground. The Swedish infantry, with prompt determination, profited by the enemy's confusion. To fill up the gaps which death had made in the front line, they formed both lines into one, and with it made the final and decisive charge. A third time they crossed the trenches, and a third time they captured the battery.

The sun was setting when the two lines closed. The strife grew hotter as it drew to an end; the last efforts of strength were mutually exerted, and skill and courage did their utmost to repair in those precious moments the fortune of the day. It was in vain; despair endows every one with superhuman strength; no one can conquer, no one will give way. The art of war seemed to exhaust its powers on one side, only to unfold some new and untried masterpiece of skill on the other. Night and darkness at last put an end to the fight, before the fury of the combatants was exhausted; and the contest only ceased when no one could any longer find an antagonist. Both armies separated, as if by tacit agreement; the trumpets sounded, and each party, claiming the victory, quitted the field. . . .

The Duke of Friedland [2] had retreated thither, and was followed on the morrow by the scattered remains of his army, without artillery, without colors, and almost without arms. The Duke of Weimar, it appears, after the toils of this bloody day, allowed the Swedish army some repose, between Lutzen and Weissenfels, near enough to the field of battle to oppose any attempt the enemy might make to recover it. Of the two armies more than nine thousand men lay dead; a still greater number were wounded, and among the Imperialists scarcely a man escaped from the field uninjured. The entire plain from Lutzen to the Canal was strewed with the wounded, the dying, and the dead. History says nothing of prisoners; a further proof of the animosity of the combatants, who neither gave nor took quarter. . . .

Duke Bernard, by keeping possession of the field, and soon after by the capture of Leipsic, maintained indisputably his claim to the title of victor. But it was a dear conquest, a dearer triumph! It was not till the fury of the contest was over that the full weight of the loss sustained was felt, and the shout of triumph died

[2] Wallenstein.

away into a silent gloom of despair. He who had led them to the charge returned not with them: there he lay upon the field which he had won, mingled with the dead bodies of the common crowd. After a long and almost fruitless search, the corpse of the King was discovered not very far from the great stone which, for a hundred years before, had stood between Lutzen and the Canal, and which, from the memorable disaster of that day, still bears the name of the "Stone of the Swede." Covered with blood and wounds, so as scarcely to be recognized, trampled beneath the horses' hoofs, stript by the rude hands of plunderers of its ornaments and clothes, his body was drawn from beneath a heap of dead, conveyed to Weissenfels, and there delivered up to the lamentations of his soldiers and the last embraces of his Queen. The first tribute had been paid to revenge, and blood had atoned for the blood of the monarch; but now affection assumed its rights, and tears of grief must flow for the man. The universal sorrow absorbs all individual woes. The generals, still stupefied by the unexpected blow, stood speechless and motionless around his bier, and no one trusted himself enough to contemplate the full extent of their loss.

II

PHILIP II AND THE NETHERLANDS [3]

OF those important political events which make the sixteenth century to take rank among the brightest of the world's epochs, the foundation of the freedom of the Netherlands appears to me one of the most remarkable. If the glittering exploits of ambition and the pernicious lust of power claim our admiration, how much more so should an event in which opprest humanity struggled for its noblest right, where with the good cause unwonted powers were united, and the resources of resolute despair triumphed in unequal contest over the terrible arts of tyranny.

Great and encouraging is the reflection that there is a resource left us against the arrogant usurpations of despotic power; that its best-contrived plans against the liberty of mankind may be frustrated; that resolute opposition can weaken even the outstretched arm of tyranny; and that heroic perseverance can eventually exhaust its fearful resources.

Never did this truth affect me so sensibly as in tracing the history of that memorable rebellion which forever severed the United Netherlands from the Spanish crown. Therefore I thought it not unworth the while to attempt to exhibit to the world this grand memorial of social union,

[3] From the introduction to the "History of the Revolt of the Netherlands." Translated by A. J. W. Morrison. This work was translated by J. Horne in 1807, and again by E. B. Eastwick in 1844.

117

in the hope that it may awaken in the breast of my reader a spirit-stirring consciousness of his own powers, and give a new and irrefragable example of what in a good cause men may both dare and venture, and what by union they may accomplish. It is not the extraordinary or heroic features of this event that induce me to describe it. The annals of the world record perhaps many similar enterprises, which may have been even bolder in the conception, and more brilliant in the execution. Some states have fallen after a nobler struggle, others have risen with more exalted strides. Nor are we here to look for eminent heroes, colossal talents, or those marvelous exploits which the history of past times presents in such rich abundance. Those times are gone, such men are no more. In the soft lap of refinement, we have suffered the energetic powers to become enervated which those ages called into action and rendered indispensable. With admiring awe, we wonder at these gigantic images of the past, as a feeble old man gazes on the athletic sports of youth.

Not so, however, in the history before us. The people here presented to our notice were the most peaceful in our quarter of the globe, and less capable than their neighbors of that heroic spirit which stamps a lofty character even on the most insignificant actions. The pressure of circumstances with its peculiar influence surprized them and forced a transitory greatness upon them, which they never could have possest, and perhaps will never possess again. It is, indeed, exactly this want of heroic grandeur which renders this event peculiarly instructive; and while others aim at showing the superiority of genius over chance, I shall here paint a scene where necessity creates genius, and accident makes heroes.

If, in any case, it be allowable to recognize the intervention of Providence in human affairs, it is certainly so in the present history, its course appears so contradictory to reason and experience. Philip II, the most powerful sovereign of his time—whose dreaded supremacy menaced the independence of Europe—whose treasures surpassed the collective wealth of all the monarchs of Christendom besides—whose ambitious projects were backed by numerous and well-disciplined armies—whose troops, hardened by long and bloody wars, and confident in past victories and in the irresistible prowess of this nation, were eager for any enterprise that promised glory and spoil, and ready to second with prompt obedience the daring genius of their leaders—this dreaded potentate here appears before us obstinately pursuing one favorite project, devoting to it the untiring efforts of a long reign, and bringing all these terrible resources to bear upon it; but forced, in the evening of his days, to abandon it—here we see the mighty Philip II engaging in combat with a few weak and powerless adversaries, and retiring from it at last with disgrace.

And with what adversaries? Here, a peaceful tribe of fishermen and shepherds, in an almost forgotten corner of Europe, which with difficulty they had rescued from the ocean; the sea their profession, and at once their wealth and their plague; poverty with freedom their highest blessing, their glory, their virtue. There, a harmless, moral commercial people, reveling in the abundant fruits of thriving industry, and jealous of the maintenance of laws which had proved their benefactors. In the happy leisure of affluence, they forsake the narrow circle of immediate wants, and learn to thirst after higher and nobler gratifications. The new views of truth whose benignant dawn now broke over Europe cast a fertilizing beam on this favored clime, and the free burgher admitted with joy the light which opprest and miserable slaves shut out. A spirit of independence, which is the ordinary companion of prosperity and freedom, lured this people on to examine the authority of antiquated opinions and to break an ignominious chain. But the stern rod of despotism was held suspended over them; arbitrary power threatened to tear away the foundation of their happiness; the guardian of their laws became their tyrant. Simple in their statecraft no less than in their manners, they dared to appeal to ancient treaties, and to remind the lord of both Indies of the right of nature. A name decides the whole issue of things. In Madrid that was called rebellion which in Brussels was simply styled a lawful remonstrance. The complaints of Brabant required a prudent mediator, Philip II sent an executioner. The signal for war was given. An unparalleled tyranny assailed both property and life. The despairing citizens, to whom the choice of deaths was all that was left, chose the nobler one on the battle-field. A wealthy and luxurious nation loves peace, but becomes warlike as soon as it becomes poor. Then it ceases to tremble for a life which is deprived of everything that had made it desirable. In an instant, the contagion of rebellion seized at once the most distant provinces; trade and commerce are at a standstill, the ships disappear from the harbors, the artizan abandons his workshop, the rustic his uncultivated fields. Thousands fled to distant lands, a thousand victims fell on the bloody field, and fresh thousands prest on. Divine, indeed, must that doctrine be for which men could die so joyfully. All that was wanting was the last finishing hand, the enlightened, enterprising spirit, to seize on this great political crisis, and to mold the offspring of chance into the ripe creation of wisdom. William the Silent, like a second Brutus, devoted himself to the great cause of liberty. Superior to all selfishness, he resigned honorable offices which entailed on him objectionable duties, and magnanimously divesting himself of all his princely dignities, he descended to a state of voluntary poverty, and became but a citizen of the world. The cause of justice was staked upon the hazardous game of battle; but the newly raised levies of mercenaries and peaceful husbandmen were unable to withstand the terrible onset of an experienced force. Twice did the brave William lead his dispirited troops against the tyrant, twice was he abandoned by them, but not by his courage.

Philip II sent as many reenforcements as the dreadful importunity of his viceroy demanded. Fugitives, whom their country rejected, sought a new home on the ocean, and turned to the ships of their enemy to satisfy the cravings both of vengeance and of want. Naval heroes were now formed out of corsairs, and a marine collected out of piratical vessels: out of morasses arose a republic. Seven provinces threw off the yoke at the same time, to form a new, youthful state, powerful by its waters and its union and despair. A solemn decree of the whole nation deposed the tyrant, and the Spanish name was erased from all its laws.

For such acts no forgiveness remained; the republic became formidable, only because it was impossible for her to retrace her steps. But factions distracted her within; without, her terrible element, the sea itself, leaguing with her oppressors, threatened her very infancy with a premature grave. She felt herself succumb to the superior force of the enemy, and cast herself a suppliant before the most powerful thrones of Europe, begging them to accept a dominion which she herself could no longer protect. At last, but with difficulty—so despised at first was this state, that even the rapacity of foreign monarchs spurned her opening bloom—a stranger deigned to accept their importunate offer of a dangerous crown. New hopes began to revive her sinking courage; but in this new father of his country destiny gave her a traitor, and in the critical emergency, when the implacable foe was in full force before her very gates, Charles of Anjou invaded the liberties which he had been called to protect. In the midst of the tempest, too, the assassin's hand tore the steersman from the helm, and with William of Orange the career of the infant republic was seemingly at an end, and all her guardian angels fled. But the ship continued to scud along before the storm, and the swelling canvas carried her safe without the pilot's help.

Philip II missed the fruits of a deed which cost him his royal honor, and perhaps, also, his self-respect. Liberty struggled on still with despotism, in obstinate and dubious contest; sanguinary battles were fought; a brilliant array of heroes succeeded each other on the field of glory; and Flanders and Brabant were the schools which educated generals for the coming century. A long, devastating war laid waste the open country; victor and vanquished alike waded through blood; while the rising republic of the waters gave a welcome to fugitive industry, and out of the ruins of despotism erected the noble edifice of its own greatness. For forty years lasted the war whose happy termination was not to bless the dying eye of Philip; which destroyed one paradise in Europe, to form a new one out of its shattered fragments; which destroyed the choicest flower of military youth, and while it enriched more than a quarter of the globe, impoverished the possessor of the golden Peru. This monarch, who could expend nine hundred tons of gold without oppressing his subjects, and by tyrannical measure extorted far more, heaped moreover on his exhausted people a debt of one hundred and forty millions of ducats. An implacable hatred of liberty swallowed up all these treasures, and consumed on the fruitless task the labor of a royal life. But the Reformation throve amidst the devastations of the sword, and over the blood of her citizens the banner of the new republic floated victorious.

AUGUST WILHELM VON SCHLEGEL

Born in 1767, died in 1845; educated at Göttingen; a tutor
for three years in Amsterdam; made professor of literature
and esthetics at Jena in 1798; founded a critical journal to
represent the Romantic school; lectured in Berlin in 1803-
04; traveled with Madame de Staël, a tutor to her children
afterward at Coppet; became secretary to the Crown Prince
Bernadotte and ennobled; professor at Bonn in 1818; visited England in 1823; wrote romances, sonnets, odes and
criticisms, and translated Shakespeare.

SHAKESPEARE'S MACBETH [1]

OF "Macbeth" I have already spoken once in
passing; and who could exhaust the praises of
this sublime work? Since the "Eumenides" of
Æschylus nothing so grand and terrible has ever
been written. The witches are not, it is true,
divine Eumenides, and are not intended to be;
they are ignoble and vulgar instruments of hell.
A German poet, therefore, very ill understood
their meaning when he transformed them into
mongrel beings, a mixture of fates, furies, and
enchantresses, and clothed them with tragic dignity. Let no man venture to lay hand on Shakespeare's works hinking to improve anything essential: he will be sure to punish himself. The
bad is radically odious, and to endeavor in any

[1] From the "Lectures on Dramatic Art and Literature."
Translated by John Black, the translation being revised by
A. J. W. Morrison. Madame de Staël heard these lectures
delivered in Vienna, and in her work on Germany says she
was "astonished to hear a critic as eloquent as an orator."

manner to ennoble it, is to violate the laws of propriety. Hence, in my opinion, Dante, and even Tasso, have been much more successful in their portraiture of demons than Milton.

Whether the age of Shakespeare still believed in ghosts and witches is a matter of perfect indifference for the justification of the use which in "Hamlet" and "Macbeth" he has made of preexisting traditions. No superstition can be widely diffused without having a foundation in human nature: on this the poet builds; he calls up from their hidden abysses that dread of the unknown, and presage of a dark side of nature, and a world of spirits, which philosophy now imagines it has altogether exploded. In this manner he is in some degree both the portrayer and the philosopher of superstition; that is, not the philosopher who denies and turns it into ridicule, but, what is still more difficult, who distinctly exhibits its origin in apparently irrational and yet natural opinions. But when he ventures to make arbitrary changes in these popular traditions he altogether forfeits his right to them, and merely holds up his idle fancies to our ridicule. Shakespeare's picture of the witches is truly magical: in the short scenes where they enter he has created for them a peculiar language, which, altho composed of the usual elements, still seems to be a collection of formulæ of incantation. The sound of the words, the accumulation of rimes, and the rhythm of the verse form, as it were, the hollow music of a dreary witch-dance. He has been abused for using the names of disgusting objects; but he who fancies the kettle of the witches can be made effective with agreeable aromatics is as wise as those who desire that hell should sincerely and honestly give good advice. These repulsive things, from which the imagination shrinks, are here emblems of the hostile powers which operate in nature; and the repugnance of our senses is outweighed by the mental horror. With one another the witches discourse like women of the very lowest class; for this was the class to which witches were ordinarily supposed to belong: when, however, they address Macbeth they assume a loftier tone: their predictions, which they either themselves pronounce, or allow their apparitions to deliver, have all the obscure brevity, the majestic solemnity, of oracles.

We here see that the witches are merely instruments; they are governed by an invisible spirit, or the operation of such great and dreadful events would be above their sphere. With what intent did Shakespeare assign the same place to them in his play which they occupy in the history of Macbeth as related in the old chronicles? A monstrous crime is committed: Duncan, a venerable old man, and the best of kings, is, in defenseless sleep, under the hospitable roof, murdered by his subject, whom he has loaded with honors and rewards. Natural motives alone seem inadequate, or the perpetrator must have been portrayed as a hardened villain. Shakespeare wished to exhibit a more sublime picture—an ambitious but noble hero yielding to a deep-laid hellish temptation, and in whom all the crimes to which, in order to secure the fruits of his first crime, he is impelled by necessity, can not altogether eradicate the stamp of native heroism.

He has, therefore, given a threefold division to the guilt of that crime. The first idea comes from that being whose whole activity is guided by a lust of wickedness.

The weird sisters surprize Macbeth in the moment of intoxication of victory, when his love of glory has been gratified; they cheat his eyes by exhibiting to him as the work of fate what in reality can be accomplished only by his own deed, and gain credence for all their words by the immediate fulfilment of the first prediction. The opportunity of murdering the King immediately offers; the wife of Macbeth conjures him not to let it slip; she urges him on with a fiery eloquence which has at command all those sophisms that serve to throw a false splendor over crime.

Little more than the mere execution falls to the share of Macbeth; he is driven into it, as it were, in a tumult of fascination. Repentance immediately follows, nay, even precedes, the deed, and the stings of conscience leave him rest neither night nor day. But he is now fairly entangled in the snares of hell; truly frightful is it to behold that same Macbeth, who once as a warrior could spurn at death, now that he dreads the prospect of the life to come, clinging with growing anxiety to his earthly existence the more miserable it becomes, and pitilessly removing out of the way whatever to his dark and suspicious mind seems to threaten danger. However much we may abhor his actions, we can not altogether refuse to compassionate the state of his mind; we lament the ruin of so many noble qualities, and even in his last defense we are compelled to admire the struggle of a brave will with a cowardly conscience. We might believe that we witness in this tragedy the overruling destiny of the ancients represented in perfect accordance with their ideas: the whole originates in a supernatural influence, to which the subsequent events seem inevitably linked. Moreover, we even find here the same ambiguous oracles which, by their literal fulfilment, deceive those who confide in them.

Yet it may be easily shown that the poet has, in his work, displayed more enlightened views. He wishes to show that the conflict of good and evil in this world can only take place by the permission of Providence, which converts the curse that individual mortals draw down on their heads into a blessing to others. An accurate scale is followed in the retaliation.

Lady Macbeth, who of all the human participators in the King's murder is the most guilty, is thrown by the terrors of her conscience into a state of incurable bodily and mental disease; she dies, unlamented by her husband, with all the symptoms of reprobation. Macbeth is still found worthy to die the death of a hero on the field of battle. The noble Macduff is allowed the satisfaction of saving his country by punishing with his own hand the tyrant who had murdered his wife and children. Banquo, by an early death, atones for the ambitious curiosity which prompted the wish to know his glorious descendants, as he thereby has roused Macbeth's jealousy; but he preserved his mind pure from the evil suggestions of the witches: his name is blest in his race, destined to enjoy for a long succession of ages that royal dignity which Macbeth could only hold for his own life. In the progress of the action, the piece is altogether the reverse of "Hamlet": it strides forward with amazing rapidity, from the first catastrophe (for Duncan's murder may be called a catastrophe) to the last. "Thought, and done!" is the general motto; for, as Macbeth says,

> "The flighty purpose never is o'ertook
> Unless the deed go with it."

In every feature we see an energetic heroic age, in the hardy north which steels every nerve. The precise duration of the action can not be ascertained—years, perhaps, according to the story—but we know that to the imagination the most crowded time appears always the shortest. Here we can hardly conceive how so very much could ever have been comprest into so narrow a space; not merely external events, the very inmost recesses of the minds of the dramatic personages are laid open to us. It is as if the drags were taken from the wheels of time and they roll along without interruption in their descent. Nothing can equal the picture in its power to excite terror. We need only allude to the circumstances attending the murder of Duncan, the dagger that hovers before the eyes of Macbeth, the vision of Banquo at the feast, the madness of Lady Macbeth: what can possibly be said on the subject that will not rather weaken the impression they naturally leave? Such scenes stand alone, and are to be found only in this poet; otherwise the tragic muse might exchange her mask for the head of Medusa.

ALEXANDER VON HUMBOLDT

Born in Berlin in 1769, died in 1859; educated at Frankfurt and Göttingen; a mining engineer in 1782; resigning his position in 1797, he traveled in Switzerland, Italy and France; made a scientific journey to South America and Mexico in 1799-1804; lived in Paris in 1809-27; settled in Berlin in 1827; went to Siberia and the Caspian Sea at the instance of the Emperor of Russia in 1829; several scientific works based on his travels appeared before 1845; in 1845-58 published his masterpiece, "Cosmos"; a brother of Frederick von Humboldt, who was a philologist.

AN ESSAY ON MAN [1]

THE general picture of nature which I have endeavored to delineate would be incomplete if I did not venture to trace a few of the most marked features of the human race, considered with reference to physical gradations—to the geographical distribution of contemporaneous types—to the influence exercised upon man by the forces of nature, and the reciprocal, altho weaker action which he, in his turn, exercises on these natural forces. Dependent, altho in a lesser degree than plants and animals, on the soil, and on the meteorological processes of the atmosphere with which he is surrounded — es-

[1] From his "General Review of Natural Phenomena" in Volume I of "Cosmos." The translation by E. C. Otté and W. S. Dallas, which came out in 1849-59. A version by Mrs. Sabine appeared in 1846; and one by Prichard in 1845-48.

caping more readily from the control of natural forces by activity of mind and the advance of intellectual cultivation no less than by his wonderful capacity of adapting himself to all climates —man everywhere becomes most essentially associated with terrestrial life. It is by these relations that the obscure and much-contested problem of the possibility of one common descent enters into the sphere embraced by a general physical cosmography. The investigation of this problem will impart a nobler, and, if I may so express myself, more purely human interest to the closing pages of this section of my work.

The vast domain of language, in whose varied structure we see mysteriously reflected the destinies of nations, is most intimately associated with the affinity of races; and what even slight differences of races may effect is strikingly manifested in the history of the Hellenic nations in the zenith of their intellectual cultivation. The most important questions of the civilization of mankind are connected with the ideas of races, community of language, and adherence to one original direction of the intellectual and moral faculties.

As long as attention was directed solely to the extremes in varieties of color and of form, and to the vividness of the first impression of the senses, the observer was naturally disposed to regard races rather as originally different species than as mere varieties. The permanence of certain types in the midst of the most hostile influences, especially of climate, appeared to favor such a view, notwithstanding the shortness of the interval of time from which the historical evidence was derived. In my opinion, however, more powerful reasons can be advanced in support of the theory of the unity of the human race, as, for instance, in the many intermediate gradations in the color of the skin and in the form of the skull, which have been made known to us in recent times by the rapid progress of geographical knowledge—the analogies presented by the varieties in the species of many wild and domesticated animals—and the more correct observations collected regarding the limits of fecundity in hybrids. The greater number of the contrasts which were formerly supposed to exist have disappeared before the laborious researches of Tiedemann on the brain of negroes and of Europeans, and the anatomical investigations of Vrolik and Weber on the form of the pelvis.

On comparing the dark-colored African nations, on whose physical history the admirable work of Prichard has thrown so much light, with the races inhabiting the islands of the South Indian and West Australian archipelago, and with the Papuas and Alfourous (Haroforas, Endamenes), we see that a black skin, woolly hair, and a negro-like cast of countenance are not necessarily connected together. So long as only a small portion of the earth was known to the Western nations, partial views necessarily predominated, and tropical heat and a black skin consequently appeared inseparable. "The Ethiopians," said the ancient tragic poet Theodectes of Phaselis, "are colored by the near sun god in his course with a sooty luster, and their hair is dried and crisped with the heat of his rays." The campaigns of Alexander, which gave rise to so many new ideas regarding physical geography, likewise first excited a discussion on the problematical influence of climate on races. "Families of animals and plants," writes one of the greatest anatomists of the day, Johannes Müller, in his noble and comprehensive work, "Physiologie des Menschen," "undergo, within certain limitations peculiar to the different races and species, various modifications in their distribution over the surface of the earth, propagating these variations as organic types of species.

"The present races of animals have been produced by the combined action of many different internal as well as external conditions, the nature of which can not in all cases be defined, the most striking varieties being found in those families which are capable of the greatest distribution over the surface of the earth. The different races of mankind are forms of one sole species, by the union of two of whose members descendants are propagated. They are not different species of a genus, since in that case their hybrid descendants would remain unfruitful. But whether the human races have descended from several primitive races of men, or from one alone, is a question that can not be determined from experience."

Geographical investigations regarding the ancient seat, the so-called cradle of the human race, are not devoid of a mythical character. "We do not know," says Wilhelm von Humboldt, in an unpublished work, "On the Varieties of Languages and Nations," "either from history or from authentic tradition, any period of time in which the human race has not been divided into social groups. Whether the gregarious condition was original, or of subsequent occurrence, we have no historic evidence to show. The separate mythical relations found to exist independently of one another in different parts of the earth appear to refute the first hypothesis, and concur in ascribing the generation of the whole human race to the union of one pair. The general prevalence of this myth has caused it to be regarded as a traditionary record transmitted from primitive man to his descendants. But this very circumstance seems rather to prove that it has no historical foundation, but has simply arisen from an identity in the mode of intellectual conception, which has everywhere led man to adopt the same conclusion regarding identical phenomena; in the same manner as many myths have doubtless arisen, not from any historical connection existing between them, but rather from an identity in human thought and imagination.

"Another evidence in favor of the purely mythical nature of this belief is afforded by the fact that the first origin of mankind—a phenomenon which is wholly beyond the sphere of experience—is explained in perfect conformity with existing views, being considered on the principle of the colonization of some desert island or remote mountainous valley at a period when mankind had already existed for thousands of years. It is in vain that we direct our thoughts to the solution of the great problem of the first origin, since man is too intimately associated with his own race and with the relations of time to conceive of the existence of an individual independently of a preceding generation and age. A solution of those difficult questions, which can not be determined by inductive reasoning or by experience—whether the belief in this presumed traditional condition be actually based on historical evidence, or whether mankind inhabited the earth in gregarious associations from the origin of the race—can not, therefore, be determined from philological data, and yet its elucidation ought not to be sought from other sources.''

The distribution of mankind is, therefore, only a distribution into varieties, which are commonly designated by the somewhat indefinite term races. As in the vegetable kingdom, and in the natural history of birds and fishes, a classification into many small families is based on a surer foundation than where large sections are separated into a few but large divisions, so it also appears to me that in the determination of races a preference should be given to the establishment of small families of nations. Whether we adopt the old classification of my master, Blumenbach, and admit five races (the Caucasian, Mongolian, American, Ethiopian, and Malayan), or that of Prichard, into seven races (the Iranian, Turanian, American, Hottentots and Bushmen, Negroes, Papuas, and Alfourous), we fail to recognize any typical sharpness of definition, or any general or well-established principle in the division of these groups. The extremes of form and color are certainly separated, but without regard to the races, which can not be included in any of these classes, and which have been alternately termed Scythian and Allophyllic. Iranian is certainly a less objectionable term for the European nations than Caucasian; but it may be maintained generally that geographical denominations are very vague when used to express the points of departure of races, more especially where the country which has given its name to the race, as, for instance, Turan (Mawerannahr), has been inhabited at different periods by Indo-Germanic and Finnish, and not by Mongolian tribes.

Languages, as intellectual creations of man, and as closely interwoven with the development of mind, are, independently of the national form which they exhibit, of the greatest importance in the recognition of similarities or differences in races. This importance is especially owing to the clue which a community of descent affords in treading that mysterious labyrinth in which the connection of physical powers and intellectual forces manifests itself in a thousand different forms. The brilliant progress made within the last half-century, in Germany, in philosophical philology, has greatly facilitated our investigations into the national character of languages and the influence exercised by descent. But here, as in all domains of ideal speculation, the dangers of deception are closely linked to the rich and certain profit to be derived.

Positive ethnographical studies, based on a thorough knowledge of history, teach us that much caution should be applied in entering into these comparisons of nations, and of the languages employed by them at certain epochs. Subjection, long association, the influence of a foreign religion, the blending of races, even when only including a small number of the more influential and cultivated of the immigrating tribes, have produced, in both continents, similarly recurring phenomena; as, for instance, in introducing totally different families of languages among one and the same race, and idioms, having one common root, among nations of the most different origin. Great Asiatic conquerors have exercised the most powerful influence on phenomena of this kind.

But language is a part and parcel of the history of the development of mind; and, however happily the human intellect, under the most dissimilar physical conditions, may unfettered pursue a self-chosen track, and strive to free itself from the dominion of terrestrial influences, this emancipation is never perfect. There ever remains, in the natural capacities of the mind, a trace of something that has been derived from the influences of race or of climate, whether they be associated with a land gladdened by cloudless azure skies, or with the vapory atmosphere of an insular region. As, therefore, richness and grace of language are unfolded from the most luxuriant depths of thought, we have been unwilling wholly to disregard the bond which so closely links together the physical world with the sphere of intellect and of the feelings by depriving this general picture of nature of those brighter lights and tints which may be borrowed from considerations, however slightly indicated, of the relations existing between races and languages. . . .

Let me close this general description of the natural phenomena of the universe. From the remotest nebulæ and from the revolving double stars, we have descended to the minutest organisms of animal creation, whether manifested in the depths of ocean or on the surface of our globe, and to the delicate vegetable germs which clothe the naked declivity of the ice-crowned mountain summit; and here we have been able to arrange these phenomena according to partially known laws; but other laws of a more mysterious nature rule the higher spheres of the organic world in which is comprized the human species in all its varied conformation, its creative intellectual power, and the languages to which it has given existence. A physical delineation of nature terminates at the point where the sphere of intellect begins, and a new world of mind is open to our view. It marks the limit, but does not pass it.

HEINRICH HEINE

Born in Prussia in 1799, died in Paris in 1856; of Hebrew
descent; with assistance from an uncle, studied jurisprudence at Bonn, Berlin, and Göttingen; embraced Christianity
in 1825; lived alternately in Hamburg, Berlin and Munich;
settled in Paris after 1831, where he spent his remaining
years; receiving, 1837-48, an annuity from the department
of foreign affairs; his first collection of poems published in
1822; his most notable prose work, "Pictures of Travel," in
1826-31; his complete works comprize twenty-one volumes.

REMINISCENCES OF NAPOLEON [1]

THE professor was dancing about the platform
with the agility of an elephant and working himself into a passion for a set tirade against the
Emperor Napoleon, when those accurst feet of
mine—no, poor feet, I can not blame you for
drumming then, nay, I could not have blamed
you had your dumb instinct thus outraged exprest itself in a yet more forcible fashion. How
can I, a pupil of Le Grand, hear the Emperor
abused? The Emperor! the great Emperor!

When I think of the great Emperor, in my
mind's eye it is summer again, all gold and green.
A long avenue of lime-trees in blossom rises up
before me; on the leafy branches sit nightingales
singing; the waterfall ripples; in the borders are
flowers dreamily waving their fair heads.

Between me and the flowers there was a strange

[1] From Chapter VII, VIII and IX, of "Travel-Pictures."
Translated by Francis Storr.

communion; the painted tulips bowed to me with the pride that apes humility, the sickly lilies nodded to me with tender sensibility, the roses with wine-flushed cheeks laughed a welcome from afar, the night-stocks sighed—with myrtles and laurels I was not then acquainted, for they had no bright blossoms to attract me, but with mignonette (we have since quarreled) I was then on the most intimate terms. I am speaking of the palace gardens at Düsseldorf, where I used to lie on the grass reverently listening to Monsieur Le Grand as he told me of the great Emperor's heroism, and beat the marches to which those heroic exploits were performed, so that my eyes and ears drank in the very life of it all. I saw the march across the Simplon—the Emperor in front and the brave grenadiers climbing up behind, while the startled eagles screamed and the glaciers thundered in the distance; I saw the Emperor clasping the standard on the bridge of Lodi; I saw the Emperor in his gray cloak at Marengo; I saw the Emperor on horseback at the battle of the Pyramids—nothing but smoke and Mamelukes—I saw the Emperor at Austerlitz—twing! how the bullets whizzed over the smooth ice—I saw, I heard the battle of Jena—dum, dum, dum—I saw, I heard the battle of Eilau, of Wagram—no, I could hardly stand it! Monsieur Le Grand drummed till my own eardrum was nearly cracked.

But what were my feelings when I saw him at last with my own eyes—O beatific vision!—himself, the Emperor.

It was in the alley of the same palace gardens at Düsseldorf. As I shouldered my way through

the gaping crowd I thought of the deeds and
battles which Monsieur Le Grand had portrayed
to me with his drum; my heart beat the grand
march—and yet I thought at the same time of the
police regulations which ordered that no one
should ride through the alley under a penalty of
five thalers. And the Emperor with his retinue
rode right through the alley! The shuddering
trees bowed down to him as he passed; the sun-
beams peeped timidly through the green foliage,
and in the blue heavens above there sailed in
sight a golden star. He wore his plain green
uniform, and his small world-famous cap. He
rode a white palfrey, which stept with such calm
pride, such assurance and dignity—had I been
the Crown Prince of Prussia, I should still have
envied that pony. Carelessly, with a loose seat,
the Emperor held up the reins in one hand, and
with the other patted good-temperedly his horse's
neck. It was a sunlit marble hand, a mighty
hand, one of those two hands that had tamed
the hydra of anarchy, and quelled the feud of
nations; and now it patted good-temperedly his
horse's neck. His face, too, was of the same
hue that we see in marble busts of Greeks and
Romans; the features wore the same expression
of calm dignity that the ancients have, and on
it was written, "Thou shalt have none other gods
but me." A smile that warmed and calmed every
heart played about his lips, and yet we know
that those lips had only to whistle and—"*la
Prusse n'existait plus*"; those lips had only to
whistle, and clericalism died like an echo; those
lips had only to whistle to set dancing the Holy
Roman Empire. And now those lips smiled, and

his eye smiled—an eye clear as heaven, an eye
that read men's hearts, an eye that at a glance
embraced all earthly things, while we mortals
see them only one by one, and only the painted
shadows. The brow was not so clear; it was
haunted by the ghosts of coming battles, and at
times a frown passed across it; these frowns
were the creative thoughts, seven-league-boot
thoughts, with which the Emperor's mind strode
invisible over the world—and I fancy each of
these thoughts would have furnished a German
writer with materials to employ his whole life.

The Emperor rode calmly down the alley; no
policeman stopt his way; behind him, on snorting
chargers, bedizened with gold and jewels, rode
his retinue; the drums beat, the trumpets blared;
at my side mad Aloysius spun round and round,
and clattered out the names of his generals;
close by drunken Gumpertz bellowed, and the
people shouted with a thousand voices, "Long
live the Emperor!"

The Emperor is dead. On a desolate island
in the Atlantic is his lonely grave, and he for
whom the earth was all too narrow rests peace-
fully beneath the hillock where five weeping wil-
lows droop their green tresses in agonized despair, and a tender-hearted rivulet ripples by
with melancholy plaint. There is no inscription
on the tombstone, but Clio has graven thereon,
in invisible letters, her just sentence that will
echo through the centuries like spirit voices.

Britannia! thou art queen of the ocean, but
all great Neptune's ocean can not wash from
thee the stain that the dead Emperor bequeathed
thee on his deathbed. Not that windbag Sir

Hudson, but thou thyself wast the Sicilian sbirro whom the allied sovereigns suborned to avenge in secret on the man of the people what the people had once done openly to one of thy sovereigns. And he was thy guest, and had seated himself at thy hearth.

To the end of all time the boys of France will talk and sing of the fell hospitality of the *Bellerophon,* and when their songs of bitter mockery are heard across the Channel the cheeks of all honorable Britons will blush with shame. But a day will come when this song will be wafted across the Straits, but not to Britain; the British nation is humbled in the dust, the tombs of the abbey are in ruins, the royal ashes they hold are forgotten; and St. Helena is the Holy Sepulcher to which the peoples of the East and of the West make pilgrimages in scarfed barks, and comfort their hearts with the great memories of the savior of the world who suffered under Hudson Lowe, as it is written in the gospels of Las Casas, of O'Meara, and of Autommarchi.

Strange, the three greatest adversaries of the Emperor have already found an awful fate. Londonderry cut his throat; Louis XVIII rotted on his throne; and Professor Sealfeld is still professor at Göttingen.

ITALY

1254—1803

MARCO POLO

Born in Venice in 1254, died in 1324; his father and uncle mercantile men whom he accompanied in 1271, when seventeen years of age, on a journey to Central Asia by way of Bagdad, and thence to the court of Kublai Khan; in 1275 entered the public service of Kublai Khan and was employed by him on important missions; left China in 1292, returning to Venice by way of India; at a battle between Venetians and Genoese, 1298, made a prisoner and confined for a year, during which he dictated in the French language to a fellow captive his book of travels; he and his father and uncle first-known Europeans to visit China.

A DESCRIPTION OF JAPAN [1]

ZIPANGU is an island in the Eastern Ocean, situated at the distance of about fifteen hundred miles [2] from the mainland, or coast of Manji. It is of considerable size; its inhabitants have fair complexions, are well made, and are civilized in their manners. Their religion is the worship of idols. They are independent of every foreign

---

[1] From the "Travels." The text of this, the most famous perhaps of all books of travel, has come down to us in an extremely corrupt state. Written as it was about 250 years before the invention of printing, innumerable copies in manuscript form were put into circulation, some in French, some in Italian, some in German and some in Latin. French is believed to be the language in which it originally was composed, but this has not been definitely proven. More than eighty copies in manuscript are still extant. A Latin version was printed in Basel in 1532. The first English translation appears to be one that was made by John Frampton, published in London in 1579. An English version by W. Marsden appeared in 1818.

[2] Chinese miles are here meant.

power, and governed only by their own kings. They have gold in the greatest abundance, its sources being inexhaustible, but, as the king does not allow of its being exported, few merchants visit the country, nor is it frequented by much shipping from other parts. To this circumstance we are to attribute the extraordinary richness of the sovereign's palace, according to what we are told by those who have access to the place. The entire roof is covered with a plating of gold, in the same manner as we cover houses, or more properly churches, with lead. The ceilings of the halls are of the same precious metal; many of the apartments have small tables of pure gold, of considerable thickness; and the windows have also golden ornaments. So vast, indeed, are the riches of the palace that it is impossible to convey an idea of them. In this island there are pearls also, in large quantities, of a red (pink) color, round in shape, and of great size, equal in value to, or even exceeding that of the white pearls. It is customary with one part of the inhabitants to bury their dead, and with another part to burn them. The former have a practise of putting one of these pearls into the mouth of the corpse. There are also found there a number of precious stones.

Of so great celebrity was the wealth of this island that a desire was excited in the breast of the grand Khan Kublai, now reigning, to make the conquest of it and to annex it to his dominions. In order to effect this he fitted out a numerous fleet, and embarked a large body of troops, under the command of two of his principal officers, one of whom was named Abbacatan,

and the other Vonsaucin. The expedition sailed
from the ports of Zai-tun and Kin-sai [probably
Amoy and Ningpo], and, crossing the intermediate sea, reached the island in safety; but in
consequence of a jealousy that arose between
the two commanders, one of whom treated the
plans of the other with contempt and resisted
the execution of his orders, they were unable to
gain possession of any city or fortified place,
with the exception of one only, which was carried by assault, the garrison having refused to
surrender. Directions were given for putting
the whole to the sword, and in obedience thereto
the heads of all were cut off, excepting of eight
persons, who, by the efficacy of a diabolical
charm, consisting of a jewel or amulet introduced
into the right arm between the skin and the
flesh, were rendered secure from the effects of
iron, either to kill or to wound. Upon this dis-
covery being made, they were beaten with a
heavy wooden club, and presently died.

It happened, after some time, that a north
wind began to blow with great force, and the
ships of the Tatars which lay near the shore
of the island were driven foul of each other.
It was determined, therefore, in a council of the
officers on board, that they ought to disengage
themselves from the land; and accordingly, as
soon as the troops were reembarked, they stood
out to sea. The gale, however, increased to so
violent a degree that a number of the vessels
foundered. The people belonging to them, by
floating on pieces of the wreck, saved themselves
upon an island lying about four miles from the
coast of Zipangu. The other ships, which, not

being so near to the land, did not suffer from the storm, and in which the two chiefs were embarked, together with the principal officers, or those whose rank entitled them to command a hundred thousand or ten thousand men, directed their course homeward, and returned to the grand khan. Those of the Tatars who remained upon the island where they were wrecked, and who amounted to about thirty thousand men, finding themselves left without shipping, abandoned by their leaders, and having neither arms nor provisions, expected nothing less than to become captives or to perish; especially as the island afforded no habitations where they could take shelter and refresh themselves. As soon as the gale ceased, and the sea became smooth and calm, the people from the main island of Zipangu came over with a large force, in numerous boats, in order to make prisoners of these shipwrecked Tatars and, having landed, proceeded in search of them, but in a straggling, disorderly manner. The Tatars, on their part, acted with prudent circumspection, and being concealed from view by some high land in the center of the island, while the enemy were hurrying in pursuit of them by one road, made a circuit of the coast by another, which brought them to the place where the fleet of boats was at anchor. Finding these all abandoned, but with their colors flying, they instantly seized them, and pushing off from the island, stood for the principal city of Zipangu, into which, from the appearance of the colors, they were suffered to enter unmolested. Here they found few of the inhabitants, besides women, whom they retained for their own use, and drove out all others.

When the King was apprized of what had taken place, he was much afflicted, and immediately gave directions for a strict blockade of the city, which was so effectual that not one person was permitted to enter or to escape from it during six months that the siege continued. At the expiration of this time, the Tatars, despairing of succor, surrendered upon the condition of their lives being spared. These events took place in the course of the year 1264 [properly 1284]. The grand khan, having learned some years after that the unfortunate issue of the expedition was to be attributed to the dissensions between the two commanders, caused the head of one of them to be cut off, and the other be sent to the savage island of Zorza, where it is the custom to execute criminals in the following manner. They are wrapt round both arms in the hide of a buffalo fresh taken from the beast, which is sewed tight. As this dries, it compresses the body to such a degree that the sufferer is incapable of moving or in any manner helping himself, and thus miserably perishes.

DANTE ALIGHIERI

Born in Florence in 1265, died in Ravenna in 1321; of an ancient family attached to the Guelph party; first saw Beatrice in his ninth year; married Gemma Donati two years after the death of Beatrice; fought with the Guelphs; entrusted with foreign missions; endeavored to reconcile Guelphs and Ghibellines; while on an embassy to Rome his house in Florence destroyed in a riot, and he condemned to exile; his life thenceforth one of wandering; settled in Ravenna in 1320, where he died a year later; all his works except "Vita Nuova" written in exile; his "Divine Comedy" in three parts written in 1300-18.

I

THAT LONG DESCENT MAKES NO MAN NOBLE[1]

HAVING confuted the errors of others in so far as they related to riches themselves we have to confute those on the subject of time as a cause of nobility, in that part where it is defined as ancient riches, and this is done in the part that begins, "Nor will they admit that a man lowly born a noble can become." And in the first place, this is refuted by an argument taken from the very people who are so mistaken; then to put them to greater confusion this, their argu-

[1] From Book IV, Chapter XIV of "The Banquet." Translated by Katharine Hillard. "The Banquet" is the least known of Dante's prose writing. It is believed to have been written in his maturity, but was not completed. Dante's purpose appears to have been to produce a sort of hand-book, or commentary, on universal knowledge.

ment, is destroyed; and this is done where it says, "And thus it comes from what I have said before." Finally it sums up—their error being evident, and it being, therefore, time to learn the truth—and this it does where it says, "Because to the healthy mind," etc.

I say then, "Nor will they admit that a man lowly born a noble can become." Here we must observe that it is the opinion of these mistaken ones that a man originally a peasant can never be called a nobleman, and a man who is the son of a peasant can likewise never be called noble. And here they contradict their own statement when they say that time is required for nobility, by putting in this word ancient (riches); because it is impossible by a process of time to arrive at the generation of nobility, by the reason of theirs here given, which denies that a man of low birth can become noble by anything he may do or by any accident; and denies the possibility of a change from a low-born father to a noble son. For if the son of a peasant be still a peasant his son also will be a peasant, and thus we can never find a point at which nobility can begin by process of time.

And if our opponent, wishing to defend himself, shall say that nobility begins at the moment when the low estate of our ancestors is forgotten, I answer that this tells against himself, because there must necessarily be a change here from the low estate to the noble, from one man to another, as from father to son, which is contrary to what they assert.

And if our opponent defends himself pertinaciously, saying that he maintains that the change may take place when the low estate of one's ancestors has fallen into oblivion, then altho the text takes no notice of this, it is fitting that the commentary should reply to it. And therefore I answer thus: that from what they say four great difficulties would follow, so that theirs can not be a good reason.

The first is that the better human nature might be the more difficult and the more tardy would be the generation of nobility, which is a great difficulty; since the better a thing is the more it is honored and the more good it causes: and nobility would be commemorated among the good things. And that this would be so is proved; for if rank or rather nobility (which is understood to be the same thing) is generated by oblivion, then the sooner men are forgotten the quicker is their nobility generated, for so much the sooner would nobility come for all. Therefore, the sooner men were forgotten, the sooner they would be ennobled, and, on the contrary, the better the memory of them the more tardy would be their nobility.

The second difficulty is that in no case except man's could such a distinction be made, that is, between noble and vile, which is a great difficulty. For in every kind of thing we see an appearance of nobility or of vileness, whence we often call one horse noble and one vile, or one falcon noble and one vile, or one pearl noble and one vile. And that this distinction could not be made is proved thus: If the forgetting of ignoble ancestors is a cause of nobility, where the ancestors never were ignoble there could be no oblivion, since oblivion is the destruction of memory. And in the said animals and plants and minerals degrees of higher and lower are not noted, because they spring from one nature and are of equal condition, and in their generation there can be nothing of nobility or the reverse, seeing that both extremes must be regarded as a possession or privation possible to the same subject; and, therefore, in them no such distinction can exist.

And if our opponent were to say that in other things nobility is understood to be the goodness therefore, but in man is understood as the forgetfulness of his low estate, one would like to answer not with words but with the knife to such stupidity as would give goodness to the cause of nobility in other things, but in man forgetfulness as its origin.

The third difficulty is that those generated would often come before the generation, which is quite impossible; and this may be demonstrated thus:

Let us suppose that Gherardo de Cammino was a grandson of the lowest peasant that ever drank of Sile or Cagnano, and that his grandfather were not yet buried in oblivion; who would dare to say that Gherardo de Cammino was not noble? And who would not agree with me in saying that he was noble? Certainly none, however presumptuous they may wish to be, because he was noble and such will his memory ever be. And if his ignoble ancestors had not been utterly forgotten (as our opponent asserts) and he had become noble and his nobility were as evident as we see it to be, then it would have existed in him before its generation had existed, and this is perfectly impossible.

The fourth difficulty is that such a man (as this supposed ancestor) would be considered noble, being dead, who was not noble when living; and a more impossible thing there could not be as may be demonstrated thus:

Let us suppose that in the age of Dardanus there remained a memory of his low-born ancestors, and let us suppose that in the age of Laomedon this memory had died out and oblivion taken its place. According to our opponent's opinion, Laomedon was noble, and Dardanus ignoble during life. Should we, to whom the memory of their ancestors (I mean beyond Dardanus) has not come down, should we say that Dardanus while alive was a common peasant, and dead became noble? And this is not contradicted by the story that he was the son of Jupiter (for this is a fable, of which, in a philosophical discussion, we should take no heed); and yet if our opponent should wish to fall back on the fable, certainly that which is covered by the fable would upset all his arguments.

And thus it is manifest that the argument of which who would make oblivion the cause of nobility is false and erroneous.

II

OF BEATRICE AND HER DEATH [2]

NINE times now, since my birth, the heaven of light had turned almost to the same point in its own gyration, when the glorious lady of my mind, who was called Beatrice by many who knew not why she was so called, first appeared before my eyes. She had already been in this life so long that in its course the starry heaven had moved toward the region of the East one of the twelve parts of a degree; so that at about the beginning of her ninth year she appeared to me, and I near the end of my ninth year saw her. She appeared to me clothed in a most noble color, a modest and becoming crimson, and she was girt and adorned in such wise as befitted her very youthful age. . . .

From that time forward Love lorded it over my soul, which had been so speedily wedded to him: and he began to exercise over me such control and such lordship, through the power which my imagination gave to him, that it behooved me to do completely all his pleasure. He commanded me ofttimes that I should seek to see this youthful angel; so that I in my boyhood often went seeking her, and saw her of such noble and praiseworthy deportment that truly of her might be said that word of the poet Homer,

[2] From "The New Life." Translated by Charles Eliot Norton. Copyright, 1867, 1892, 1895, by Houghton Mifflin Company.

"She seems not the daughter of mortal man, but of God." And tho her image, which stayed constantly with me, gave assurance to Love to hold lordship over me, yet it was of such noble virtue that it never suffered Love to rule me without the faithful counsel of the reason in those matters in which it was useful to hear such counsel. And since to dwell upon the passions and actions of such early youth seems like telling an idle tale, I will leave them, and, passing over many things which might be drawn from the original where these lie hidden, I will come to those words which are written in my memory under larger paragraphs.

When so many days had passed that nine years were exactly complete since the above-described apparition of this most gentle lady, on the last of these days it happened that this admirable lady appeared to me, clothed in purest white, between two gentle ladies, who were of greater age; and, passing along a street, she turned her eyes toward that place where I stood very timidly, and by her ineffable courtesy, which is to-day rewarded in the eternal world, saluted me with such virtue that it seemed to be then that I saw all the bounds of bliss. . . . And since it was the first time that her words came to my ears, I took in such sweetness that, as it were, intoxicated, I turned away from the folk, and betaking myself to the solitude of my own chamber, I sat myself down to think of this most courteous lady.

Then it came to pass that, walking on a road alongside of which was flowing a very clear stream, so great a desire to say somewhat in verse came upon me, that I began to consider the method I should observe; and I thought that to speak of her would not be becoming unless I were to speak to ladies in the second person; and not to every lady, but only to those who are gentle, and are not women merely. Then I say that my tongue spoke as if moved of its own accord, and said, Ladies that have the intelligence of Love. These words I laid up in my mind with great joy, thinking to take them for my beginning; wherefore then, having returned to the above-mentioned city, after some days of thought, I began a canzone with this beginning.

This most gentle lady came into such favor among the people that when she passed along the way, persons ran to see her; which gave me wonderful joy. And when she was near any one, such modesty came into his heart that he dared not raise his eyes, or return her salutation; and of this many, as having experienced it, could bear witness for me to whoso might not believe it. She, crowned and clothed with humility, took her way, showing no pride in that which she saw and heard. Many said, when she had passed: "This is not a woman; rather she is one of the most beautiful angels of heaven." And others said: "She is a marvel. Blest be the Lord who can work thus admirably!" I say that she showed herself so gentle and so full of all pleasantness that those who looked on her comprehended in themselves a pure and sweet delight, such as they could not after tell in words; nor was there any who might look upon her but that at first he needs must sigh. These and more admirable things proceeded from her admirably and with power. Wherefore I, thinking upon this, desiring to resume the style of her praise, resolved to say words in which I would set forth her admirable and excellent influences, to the end that not only those who might actually behold her, but also others should know of her whatever words could tell. . . .

I was yet full of the design of this canzone, and had completed [one] stanza thereof, when the Lord of Justice called this most gentle one to glory, under the banner of that holy Queen Mary, whose name was ever spoken with greatest reverence by this blest Beatrice.

On that day on which the year was complete since this lady was made one of the denizens of life eternal, I was seated in a place where, having her in mind, I was drawing an angel upon certain tablets. And while I was drawing it, I turned my eyes and saw at my side men to whom it was meet to do honor. They were looking on what I did, and, as was afterward told me, they had been there already some time before I became aware of it. When I saw them I rose, and saluting them, said, "Another was just now with me, and on that account I was in thought." And when they had gone away, I returned to my work, namely, that of drawing figures of angels; and while doing this, a thought came to me of saying words in rime, as if for an anniversary poem of her, and of addressing those persons who had come to me.

After this, two gentle ladies sent to ask me to send them some of these rimed words of mine; wherefore I, thinking on their nobleness, resolved to send to them and to make a new thing which

I would send to them with these, in order that I might fulfil their prayers with the more honor. And I devised then a sonnet which relates my condition, and I sent it to them. . . .

After this a wonderful vision appeared to me, in which I saw things which made me resolve to speak no more of the blest one, until I could more worthily treat of her. And to attain to this, I study to the utmost of my power, as she truly knows. So that, if it shall please Him through whom all things live that my life be prolonged for some years, I hope to say of her what was never said of any woman.

And then may it please Him who is the Lord of Grace, that my soul may go to behold the glory of its lady, namely of that blest Beatrice, who in glory looks upon the face of Him *qui est per omnia sæcula benedictus* [who is blest forever].

FRANCIS PETRARCH

Born in 1304, died in 1374; his father banished from
Florence at the same time as Dante; settled at Avignon in
1313; studied at Montpelier; first saw the Laura of his sonnets in 1327; became a canon at Lombez in 1335; settled
at Vaucluse in 1337, where he wrote his best works; called
both to Rome and Paris in 1340 to be crowned poet laureate; settled in Milan in 1353; employed on various diplomatic missions; removed to Padua in 1362; met Boccaccio in
Venice in 1362, for the last time; besides his sonnets, odes
and other poems, wrote controversial and polemical treatises,
letters and orations.

OF GOOD AND EVIL FORTUNE[1]

WHEN I consider the instability of human
affairs and the variations of fortune, I find nothing more uncertain or restless than the life of
man. Nature has given to animals an excellent
remedy under disasters, which is the ignorance
of them. We seem better treated in intelligence,
foresight, and memory. No doubt these are admirable presents; but they often annoy more than
they assist us. A prey to unuseful or distressing
cares, we are tormented by the present, the
past, and the future; and, as if we feared we
should not be miserable enough, we join to the
evil we suffer the remembrance of a former distress and the apprehension of some future ca-

[1] From the "Treatise on the Remedies of Good and Bad
Fortune." An English translation of this work under the
title "Phisicke Against Fortune," made by Thomas Twyne,
was published in London in 1579.

lamity. This is the Cerberus with three heads we combat without ceasing. Our life might be gay and happy if we would; but we eagerly seek subjects of affliction to render it irksome and melancholy. We pass the first years of this life in the shades of ignorance, the succeeding ones in pain and labor, the latter part in grief and remorse, and the whole in error; nor do we suffer ourselves to possess one bright day without a cloud.

Let us examine this matter with sincerity, and we shall agree that our distresses chiefly arise from ourselves. It is virtue alone which can render us superior to Fortune; we quit her standard, and the combat is no longer equal. Fortune mocks us; she turns us on her wheel: she raises and abases us at her pleasure, but her power is founded on our weakness. This is an old-rooted evil, but it is not incurable: there is nothing a firm and elevated mind can not accomplish. The discourse of the wise and the study of good books are the best remedies I know of; but to these we must join the consent of the soul, without which the best advice will be useless. What gratitude do we not owe to those great men who, tho dead many ages before us, live with us by their works, discourse with us, are our masters and guides, and serve us as pilots in the navigation of life, where our vessel is agitated without ceasing by the storms of our passions! It is here that true philosophy brings us to a safe port, by a sure and easy passage; not like that of the schools, which, raising us on its airy and deceitful wings, and causing us to hover on the clouds of frivolous dispute, let us fall without any light or instruction in the same place where she took us up.

Dear friend, I do not attempt to exhort you to the study I judge so important. Nature has given you a taste for all knowledge, but Fortune has denied you the leisure to acquire it; yet, whenever you could steal a moment from public affairs, you sought the conversation of wise men; and I have remarked that your memory often served you instead of books. It is therefore unnecessary to invite you to do what you have always done; but, as we can not retain all we hear or read, it may be useful to furnish your mind with some maxims that may best serve to arm you against the assaults of misfortune. The vulgar, and even philosophers, have decided that adverse fortune was most difficult to sustain. For my own part I am of a different opinion, and believe it more easy to support adversity than prosperity; and that fortune is more treacherous and dangerous when she caresses than when she dismays. Experience has taught me this, not books or arguments. I have seen many persons sustain great losses, poverty, exile, tortures, death, and even disorders that were worse than death with courage; but I have seen none whose heads have not been turned by power, riches, and honors. How often have we beheld those overthrown by good fortune who could never be shaken by bad! This made me wish to learn how to support a great fortune. You know the short time this work has taken. I have been less attentive to what might shine than to what might be useful on this subject. Truth and virtue are the wealth of all men; and shall I not discourse on these with my dear Azon? I would prepare for you, as in a little portable box, a friendly antidote against the poison of good and bad fortune. The one requires a rein to repress the sallies of a transported soul; the other a consolation to fortify the overwhelmed and afflicted spirit.

Nature gave you, my friend, the heart of a king, but she gave you not a kingdom, of which therefore Fortune could not deprive you. But I doubt whether our ages can furnish an example of worse or better treatment from her than yourself. In the first part of your life you were blest with an admirable constitution and astonishing health and vigor: some years after we beheld you thrice abandoned by the physicians, who despaired of your life. The heavenly Physician, who was your sole resource, restored your health, but not your former strength. You were then called iron-footed, for your singular force and agility; you are now bent, and lean upon the shoulders of those whom you formerly supported. Your country beheld you one day its governor, the next an exile. Princes disputed for your friendship, and afterward conspired your ruin. You lost by death the greatest part of your friends; the rest, according to custom, deserted you in calamity. To these misfortunes was added a violent disease, which attacked you when destitute of all succors, at a distance from your country and family, in a strange land, invested by the troops of your enemies; so that those two or three friends whom fortune had left you could not come near to relieve you. In a word, you have experienced every hardship but imprisonment and death. But what do I say? You have felt all the horrors of the former, when your faithful wife and children were shut up by your enemies; and even death followed you, and took one of those children, for whose life you would willingly have sacrificed your own.

In you have been united the fortunes of Pompey and Marius; but you were neither arrogant in prosperity as the one, nor discouraged in adversity as the other. You have supported both in a manner that has made you loved by your friends and admired by your enemies. There is a peculiar charm in the serene and tranquil air of virtue, which enlightens all around it, in the midst of the darkest scenes and the greatest calamities. My ancient friendship for you has caused me to quit everything for you to perform a work, in which, as in a glass, you may adjust and prepare your soul for all events; and be able to say, as Æneas did to the Sibyl, "Nothing of this is new to me; I have foreseen, and am prepared for it all." I am sensible that, in the disorders of the mind, as well as those of the body, discourses are not thought the most efficacious remedies; but I am persuaded also that the malady of the soul ought to be cured by spiritual application.

If we see a friend in distress, and give him all the consolation we are able, we perform the duties of friendship, which pays more attention to the disposition of the heart than the value of the gift. A small present may be the testimony of a great love. There is no good I do not wish you, and this is all I can offer toward it. I wish this little treatise may be of use to you.

GIOVANNI BOCCACCIO

Born in Italy probably in 1313, died in 1375; lived in
Florence in his youth; settled at Naples in 1330; returned
to Florence about 1341, where he lectured on Dante; several
times sent abroad as ambassador; his chief work the "De-
cameron," comprising one hundred stories published collectively in 1353; wrote many other works of fiction and history, some being in Latin.

THE PATIENT GRISELDA [1]

HE [the Marquis of Saluzzo] had taken a
fancy, some time before, to the behavior of a
poor country girl, who lived in a village not
far from his palace; and thinking he might live
comfortably enough with her, he determined,

[1] This, the most famous of Boccaccio's stories, is the last
of those related on the tenth day. Lowndes's "Manual"
mentions under Boccaccio "the Booke called de John Bochas,
descriving the Falle of Princis and Princessis and Other
Nobles, traslated into Englisshe by John Lydgate, Folio, London, 1494." Another early translation appeared in 1560,
but this appears to have contained parts only of the "De-
cameron." An edition issued in 1620-25 is called by Lowndes "the first English translation," by which apparently is
meant the first complete one. A translation by E. Dubois
was issued in 1806. Boccaccio's Tales were known in England before the invention of printing. Chaucer, who made
use of the story of Griselda, has told as follows how he first
obtained it from Petrarch in Padua.

> "I wolle you telle a tale which that I
> Lernid at Padow of a worthie clerke,
> Fraucis Petrarke, the laureate poete."

without seeking any further, to marry her. . . .
The people all declared themselves pleased, and
promised to regard her in all things as their
mistress. Afterward they made preparations for
a most noble feast, and the like did the prince,
inviting all his relations, and the great lords in
all parts and provinces about him; he had also
most rich and costly robes made, shaped by a
person that seemed to be of the same size with
his intended spouse; and provided a girdle, ring,
and fine coronet, with everything requisite for
a bride. And when the day appointed was come,
about the third hour he mounted his horse, attended by all his friends and vassals, and, having
everything in readiness, he said, "My lords and
gentlemen, it is now time to go for my new
spouse."

So on they rode to the village, and when he
was come near the father's house he saw her
carrying some water from the well, in great
haste to go afterward with some of her acquaint-
ances to see the new marchioness; when he called
her by her name, which was Griselda, and inquired where her father was. She modestly replied, "My gracious lord, he is in the house."
He then alighted from his horse, commanding
them all to wait for him, and went alone into
the cottage, where he found the father, who was
called Giannucolo, and said to him, "Honest man,
I am come to espouse thy daughter, but would
first ask her some questions before thee." He
then inquired whether she would make it her
study to please him, and not be uneasy at any
time, whatever he should do or say; and whether
she would always be obedient; with more to that

purpose. To which she answered, "Yes." He then led her out by the hand, and, ordering the rich apparel to be brought which he had provided, he had her clothed completely, and a coronet set upon her head, all disordered as her hair was; after which, every one being in amaze, he said, "Behold, this is the person whom I intend for my wife, provided she will accept of me for her husband." Then, turning toward her, who stood quite abashed, "Will you," said he, "have me for your husband?" She replied, "Yes, if it so please your lordship." "Well," he replied, "and I take you for my wife."

So he espoused her in that public manner, and, mounting her on a palfrey, conducted her honorably to his palace, celebrating the nuptials with as much pomp and grandeur as tho he had been married to the daughter of the King of France; and the young bride showed apparently that with her garments she had changed both her mind and behavior. She had a most agreeable person, and was so amiable, and so good-natured withal, that she seemed rather a lord's daughter than a poor shepherd's; at which every one that knew her before was greatly surprized. She was so obedient, also, to her husband, and so obliging in all respects, that he thought himself the happiest man in the world; and to her subjects likewise so gracious and condescending that they all honored and loved her as their own lives, praying for her health and prosperity, and declaring, contrary to their former opinion, that Gualtieri was the most prudent and sharp-sighted prince in the whole world; for that no one could have discerned such virtues under a mean habit and a country disguise but himself. In a very short time her discreet behavior and good works were the common subject of discourse, not in that country alone, but everywhere else; and what had been objected to the prince, with regard to his marrying her, now took a contrary turn. They had not lived long together before she proved with child, and at length brought forth a daughter, for which he made great rejoicings.

But soon afterward a new fancy came into his head, and that was to make trial of her patience by long and intolerable sufferings: so he began with harsh words and an appearance of great uneasiness—telling her that his subjects were greatly displeased with her for her mean parentage, especially as they saw she bore children, and that they did nothing but murmur at the daughter already born. Which when she heard, without changing countenance or her resolution in any respect, she replied, "My lord, pray dispose of me as you think most for your honor and happiness: I shall entirely acquiesce, knowing myself to be meaner than the meanest of the people, and that I was altogether unworthy of that dignity to which your favor was pleased to advance me."

This was very agreeable to the prince, seeing that she was in no way elevated with the honor he had conferred upon her. Afterward, having often told her, in general terms, that his subjects could not bear with the daughter that was born of her, he sent one of his servants, whom he had instructed what to do, who, with a very sorrowful countenance, said to her, "Madam, I must either lose my own life or obey my lord's commands; now he has ordered me to take your daughter, and—'' without saying anything more. She, hearing these words, and noting the fellow's looks, remembering also what she had heard before from her lord, concluded that he had orders to destroy the child. So she took it out of the cradle, kissed it, and gave it her blessing; when, without changing countenance, tho her heart throbbed with maternal affection, she tenderly laid it in the servant's arms, and said, "Take it, and do what thy lord and mine has commanded; but, prithee, leave it not to be devoured by the fowls or wild beasts, unless that be his will." Taking the child, he acquainted the prince with what she said, who was greatly surprized at her constancy; and he sent the same person with it to a relation at Bologna, desiring her, without revealing whose child it was, to see it carefully brought up and educated. Afterward the lady became with child a second time, and was delivered of a son, at which he was extremely pleased.

But, not satisfied with what he had already done, he began to grieve and persecute her still more, saying one day to her, seemingly much out of temper, "Since thou hast brought me this son, I am able to live no longer with my people; for they mutiny to that degree that a poor shepherd's grandson is to succeed, and be their lord after me, that, unless I would run the risk of being driven out of my dominions, I must needs dispose of this child as I did of the other, and then send thee away, in order to take a wife more suitable to me." She heard this with a great deal of resignation, making only this reply: "My lord, study only your own ease and happiness, without the least care for me; for nothing is agreeable to me but what is pleasing to yourself.'' Not many days after he sent for the son in the same manner as he had done for the daughter, and seeming also as if he had procured him to be destroyed, had him conveyed to Bologna, to be taken care of with the daughter. This she bore with the same resolution as before, at which the prince wondered greatly, declaring to himself that no other woman was capable of doing the like. And were it not that he had observed her extremely fond of her children, while that was agreeable to him, he should have thought it want of affection in her; but he saw it was only her entire obedience and condescension. The people, imagining that the children were both put to death, blamed him to the last degree, thinking him the most cruel and worst of men, and showing great compassion for the lady, who, whenever she was in company with the ladies of her acquaintance, and they condoled with her for her loss, would only say, ''It was not my will, but his who begot them.''

But more years being now passed, and he resolving to make the last trial of her patience, declared, before many people, that he could no longer bear to keep Griselda as his wife, owning that he had done very foolishly, and like a young man, in marrying her, and that he meant to solicit the pope for a dispensation to take another and send her away; for which he was much blamed by many worthy persons; but he said nothing in return, only that it should be so. She, hearing this, and expecting to go home to her father's, and possibly tend the cattle as she had done before, while she saw some other lady possest of him, whom she dearly loved and honored, was perhaps secretly grieved; but as she had withstood other strokes of fortune, so she determined resolutely to do now. Soon afterward Gualtieri had counterfeit letters come to him, as from Rome, acquainting all his people that his holiness thereby dispensed with his marrying another and turning away Griselda. He then brought her before him, and said, "Woman, by the pope's leave I may dispose of thee, and take another wife. As my ancestors, then, have been all sovereign princes of this country, and thine only peasants, I intend to keep thee no longer, but to send thee back to thy father's cottage, with the same fortune which thou broughtest me, and afterward to make choice of one more suitable in quality to myself." It was with the utmost difficulty she could now refrain from tears; and she replied, "My lord, I was always sensible that my servile condition would no way accord with your high rank and descent. For what I have been, I own myself indebted to Providence and you; I considered it as a favor lent me: you are now pleased to demand it back; I therefore willingly restore it. Behold the ring with which you espoused me; I deliver it you. You bid me take the dowry back which I brought you; you will have no need for a teller to count it, nor I for a purse to put it in, much less a sumpter horse to carry it away." . . . So she left his palace in that manner, and returned weeping to her father's, to the great grief of all who saw her.

The poor man, never supposing that the prince would keep her so long as his wife, and expecting this thing to happen every day, safely laid up the garments of which she had been despoiled the day he espoused her. He now brought them to her, and she put them on, and went as usual about her father's little household affairs, bearing this fierce trial of adverse fortune with the greatest courage imaginable. The prince then gave out that he was to espouse a daughter of one of the counts of Panago; and, seeming as if he made great preparations for his nuptials, he sent for Griselda to come to him, and said to her, "I am going to bring this lady home whom I have just married and intend to show her all possible respect at her first coming: thou knowest that I have no woman with me able to set out the rooms, and do many other things which are requisite on so solemn an occasion. As, therefore, thou art best acquainted with the state of the house, I would have thee make such provision as thou shalt judge proper, and invite what ladies thou wilt, even as tho thou wert mistress of the house, and when the marriage is ended get thee home to thy father's again." Tho these words pierced like daggers to the heart of Griselda, who was unable to part with her love for the prince so easily as she had done with her great fortune, yet she replied, "My lord, I am ready to fulfil all your commands." She then went in her coarse attire into the palace, and with her own hands did she begin to sweep, and set all the rooms to rights, cleaning the stools and benches in the hall like the meanest servant, and directing what was to be done in the kitchen, never giving over till everything was in order and as it ought to be. After this was done she invited, in the prince's name, all the ladies in the country to come to the feast. And on the day appointed for the marriage, meanly clad as she was, she received them in the most genteel and cheerful manner imaginable.

Now, Gualtieri, who had his children carefully brought up at Bologna (the girl being about twelve years old, and one of the prettiest creatures that ever was seen, and the boy six), had sent to his kinswoman there, to desire she would bring them, with an honorable retinue, to Saluzzo, giving it out all the way she came, that she was bringing the young lady to be married to him, without letting any one know to the contrary. Accordingly, they all three set forward, attended by a goodly train of gentry, and, after some days' traveling, reached Saluzzo about dinner-time, when they found the whole company assembled, waiting to see their new lady. The young lady was most graciously received by all the women present, and being come into the hall where the tables were all covered, Griselda, meanly drest as she was, went cheerfully to meet her, saying, ''Your ladyship is most kindly welcome.'' The ladies, who had greatly importuned the prince, tho to no purpose, to let Griselda be in a room by herself, or else that she might have some of her own clothes, and not appear before strangers in that manner, were now seated, and going to be served round, while the young lady was universally admired, and every one said that the prince had made a good change; but Griselda, in particular, highly commended both her and her brother. The marquis now thinking that he had seen enough with regard to his wife's patience, and perceiving that in all her trials she was still the same, being persuaded, likewise, that this proceeded from no want of understanding in her, because he knew her to be singularly prudent, he thought it time to take her from that anguish which he supposed she might conceal under her firm and constant deportment. So, making her come before all the company, he said, with a smile, "What thinkest thou, Griselda, of my bride?" "My lord," she replied, "I like her extremely well; and if she be as prudent as she is fair, you may be the happiest man in the world with her: but I most humbly beg that you would not take those heart-breaking measures with this lady as you did with your last wife, because she is young and has been tenderly educated, whereas the other was inured to hardships from a child."

Gualtieri perceiving that, tho Griselda thought that person was to be his wife, she nevertheless answered him with great humility and sweetness of temper, he made her sit down by him, and said, "Griselda, it is now time for you to reap the fruit of your long patience, and that they who have reputed me to be cruel, unjust, and a monster in nature may know that what I have done has been all along with a view to teach you how to behave as a wife; to show them how to choose and keep a wife; and, lastly, to secure my own ease and quiet as long as we live together, which I was apprehensive might have been endangered by my marrying. Therefore I had a mind to prove you by harsh and injurious treatment; and, not being sensible that you have ever transgrest my will, either in word or deed, I now seem to have met with that happiness I desired. I intend, then, to restore in one hour what I have taken away from you in many, and to make you the sweetest recompense for the many bitter pangs I have caused you to suffer. Accept, therefore, this young lady, whom thou thought my spouse, and her brother, as your children and mine. They are the same whom you, and many others believed that I had been the means of cruelly murdering; and I am your husband, who love and value you above all things, assuring myself that no person in the world can be happier in a wife than I am."

With this he embraced her most affectionately, when, rising up together (she weeping for joy), they went where their daughter was sitting, quite astonished with these things, and tenderly saluted both her and her brother, undeceiving them and the whole company. At this the women all arose, overjoyed, from the tables, and, taking Griselda into the chamber, they clothed her with her own noble apparel, and as a marchioness, resembling such a one even in rags, and brought her into the hall. And being extremely rejoiced with her son and daughter, and every one expressing the utmost satisfaction at what had come to pass, the feasting was prolonged many days. The marquis was adjudged a very wise man, tho. abundantly too severe, and the trial of his lady most intolerable; but as for Griselda, she was beyond compare.

NICCOLO MACHIAVELLI

Born in Florence in 1469, died in 1527; of a noble but impoverished family; employed in diplomatic missions to small Italian states and France and Germany; deprived of office when the Medici returned to Florence in 1512; imprisoned and tortured in 1513 on suspicion of being a conspirator; retired to a country estate, where he took up literary work; author of "The Prince," "The History of Florence," essays and comedies.

OUGHT PRINCES TO KEEP THEIR PROMISES [1]

IT is unquestionably very praiseworthy in princes to be faithful to their engagements; but among those of the present day, who have been distinguished for great exploits, few indeed have been remarkable for this virtue, or have scrupled

[1] From Chapter XVIII of "The Prince." Machiavelli's writings appear not to have been translated into English until some years had elapsed after his death. The first work mentioned by Lowndes is "The Arte of Warre," as "set forth in Englisshe" by Peter Whitehaorne, published in 1560. Another translation appeared in 1608, under the title "Discourse upon the Meanes of wei Governing and Maintaining in good peace a Kingdome." A more modern translation is by Ellis Farnsworth. The most recent of all, by Christian E. Detmold, was published in Boston in 1882.

The earliest English translation of the "History of Florence" appears to be one made by Thomas Bedingfield, published in 1594. Another early translation was issued in 1675. In 1752 the translation by Ellis Farnsworth was published.

to deceive others who may have relied on their good faith.

It should, therefore, be known that there are two ways of deciding any contest; the one by laws, the other by force. The first is peculiar to men, the second to beasts; but when laws are not sufficiently powerful, it is necessary to recur to force; a prince ought, therefore, to understand how to use both these descriptions of arms. This doctrine is admirably illustrated to us by the ancient poets in the allegorical history of the education of Achilles, and many other princes of antiquity, by the centaur Chiron, who, under the double form of man and beast, taught those who were destined to govern that it was their duty to use by turns the arms adapted to both these natures, seeing that one without the other can not be of any durable advantage. Now, as a prince must learn how to act the part of a beast sometimes, he should make the fox and the lion his patterns. The first can but feebly defend himself against the wolf, and the latter readily falls into such snares as are laid for him. From the fox, therefore, a prince will learn dexterity in avoiding snares; and from the lion how to employ his strength to keep the wolves in awe. But they who entirely rely upon the lion's strength, will not always meet with success; in other words, a prudent prince can not and ought not to keep his word, except when he can do it without injury to himself, or when the circumstances under which he contracted the engagement still exist.

I should be cautious in inculcating such a precept if all men were good; but as the generality of mankind are wicked, and ever ready to break their words, a prince should not pique himself in keeping his more scrupulously, especially as it is always easy to justify a breach of faith on his part. I could give numerous proofs of this, and show numberless engagements and treaties which have been violated by the treachery of princes, and that those who enacted the part of the fox have always succeeded best in their affairs. It is necessary, however, to disguise the appearance of craft, and thoroughly to understand the art of feigning and dissembling; for men are generally so simple and so weak that he who wishes to deceive easily finds dupes.

One example, taken from the history of our own times, will be sufficient. Pope Alexander VI played during his whole life a game of deception; and notwithstanding his faithless conduct was extremely well known, his artifices always proved successful. Oaths and protestations cost him nothing; never did a prince so often break his word or pay less regard to his engagements. This was because he so well understood this chapter in the art of government.

It is not necessary, however, for a prince to possess all the good qualities I have enumerated, but it is indispensable that he should appear to have them. I will even venture to affirm that it is sometimes dangerous to use, tho it is always useful to seem to possess them. A prince should earnestly endeavor to gain the reputation of kindness, clemency, piety, justice, and fidelity to his engagements. He ought to possess all these good qualities, but still retain such power over himself as to display their opposites whenever it may be expedient. I maintain that a prince, and especially a new prince, can not with impunity exercise all the virtues, because his own self-preservation will often compel him to violate the laws of charity, religion, and humanity. He should habituate himself to bend easily to the various circumstances which may from time to time surround him. In a word, it will be as useful to him to persevere in the path of rectitude, while he feels no inconvenience in doing so, as to know how to deviate from it when circumstances dictate such a course. He should make it a rule, above all things, never to utter anything which does not breathe of kindness, justice, good faith, and piety; this last quality it is most important for him to appear to possess, as men in general judge more from appearance than from reality. All men have eyes, but few have the gift of penetration. Every one sees your exterior, but few can discern what you have in your heart; and those few dare not oppose the voice of the multitude, who have the majesty of their prince on their side. Now, in forming a judgment of the minds of men, and more especially of princes, as we can not recur to any tribunal, we must attend only to results. Let it then be the prince's chief care to maintain his authority; the means he employs, be what they may, will, for this purpose, always appear honorable and meet applause; for the vulgar are ever caught by appearances, and judge only by the event. And as the world is chiefly composed of such as are called the vulgar, the voice of the few is seldom or never heard or regarded.

BENVENUTO CELLINI

Born in Florence in 1500, died in 1571; worked in Pisa from 1516 to 1517; in Rome from 1523-40; assisted in the defense of the castle of St. Angelo during the siege and sacking of Rome by the Constable De Bourbon in 1527; imprisoned in St. Angelo in 1528, his account of his escape being the gem of his "Autobiography"; in France at the court of Francis I in 1540-44; in Florence ser ing the Medici, 1544-71, and for them produced the Perseus now standing in Florence; his "Autobiography" not printed until 1730, altho well known previously in manuscript form.

THE CASTING OF HIS "PERSEUS AND MEDUSA"[1]

As I had been particularly successful in casting my Medusa, I made a model of my Perseus in wax, and flattered myself that I should have the same success in casting the latter in bronze as I had had with the former. Upon its appearing to such advantage and looking so beautiful in wax, the duke,[2] whether somebody else put it into his head, or whether it was a notion of his own, as he came to my house oftener than usual,

---

[1] From the "Autobiography," as translated in 1822 by William Roscoe, the Liverpool banker and man of letters, who wrote a well-known "Life of Leo X," and of whom Irving, in his "Sketch Book," has left a pathetic personal account. The earliest English translation of Cellini appears to have been made by Thomas Nugent and published in 1771. The latest is by John Addington Symonds.

[2] The reference is to Cosmo dei Medici, then ruler of Florence.

once took occasion to say to me, "Benvenuto, this statue can not be cast in bronze: it is not in the power of your art to compass it." Hearing him express himself in that manner, I discovered great vexation, and said, "My lord, I know that your excellency places very little confidence in me, and that you have but too good an opinion of those who speak ill of me; or else you do not understand things of this nature." Scarce did he suffer me to utter these words when he answered, "I profess to understand them, and I do understand them perfectly." I replied, "You may understand them as a prince, but not as an artist; for if you had that skill in these matters which you think you have, you would believe me on account of that fine bronze head which I cast for your excellency, and which was sent to the Elbe; as also for having restored the beautiful figure of Ganymede, a work that gave me infinite trouble, insomuch that it would have been easier for me to have made a new one; likewise for having cast the Medusa, which stands here before your excellency, a performance of immense difficulty, in which I have done what no other man has done before me in this most laborious art." . . .

The duke scarcely had patience to hear me out, but sometimes turned one way, sometimes another; and I was quite in despair when I recollected the circumstances in which I had lived in France. At last he all of a sudden said, "Tell me, Benvenuto, how is it possible that this fine head of Medusa, which Perseus holds aloft in his hand, should ever come out cleverly?" I immediately answered, "It is clear, my lord, that you are no connoisseur in statuary, as your excellency boasts yourself; for if you had any skill in the art, you would not be afraid of that fine head not coming out, but would express your apprehensions concerning that right foot, which is at such a distance below.'' The duke, half-angry, addressing himself to some noblemen who were with him, said, ''I really believe it is a practise of Benvenuto's to contradict and oppose everything he hears advanced.'' . . .

After I had made its coat of earth, covered it well, and bound it properly with irons, I began by means of a slow fire to draw off the wax, which melted away by many ventholes; for the more of these are made, the better the molds are filled; and when I had entirely stript off the wax, I made a sort of fence around my Perseus, that is, round the mold above mentioned, of bricks, piling them one upon another, and leaving several vacuities for the fire to exhale at. I next began gradually to put on the wood, and kept a constant fire for two days and two nights, till, the wax being quite off, and the mold well baked, I began to dig a hole to bury my mold in, and observed all those fine methods of proceeding that are prescribed by our art. When I had completely dug my hole, I took my mold, and by means of levers and strong cables directed it with care, and suspended it a cubit above the level of the furnace, so that it hung exactly in the middle of the hole. I then let it gently down to the very bottom of the furnace, and placed it with all the care and exactness I possibly could.

After I had finished this part of my task, I began to make a covering of the very earth I had taken off, and in proportion as I raised the earth I made vents for it, which are a sort of tubes of baked earth, generally used for conduits, and other things of a similar nature. As soon as I saw that I had placed it properly, and that this manner of covering it, by putting on these small tubes in their proper places, was likely to answer, as also that my journeymen thoroughly understood my plan, which was very different from that of all other masters, and I was sure that I could depend upon them, I turned my thoughts to my furnace. I had caused it to be filled with several pieces of brass and bronze, and heaped them upon one another in the manner taught us by our art, taking particular care to leave a passage for the flames, that the metal might the sooner assume its color and dissolve into a fluid. Thus I with great alacrity excited my men to lay on the pine wood, which, because of the oiliness of the resinous matter that oozes from the pine-tree, and that my furnace was admirably well made, burned at such a rate that I was continually obliged to run to and fro, which greatly fatigued me. I, however, bore the hardship; but, to add to my misfortune, the shop took fire, and we were all very much afraid the roof would fall in and crush us. From another quarter, that is, from the garden, the sky poured in so much rain and wind that it cooled my furnace.

Thus did I continue to struggle with these cross accidents for several hours, and exerted myself to such a degree that my constitution, tho robust, could no longer bear such severe hardship, and I was suddenly attacked by a most violent intermitting fever: in short, I was so ill that I found myself under a necessity of lying down upon my bed. . . .

My housekeeper, whose name was Mona Fiora da Castel del Rio, was one of the most sensible and affectionate women in the world: she rebuked me for giving way to vain fears, and at the same time attended me with the greatest kindness and care imaginable; however, seeing me so very ill, and terrified to such a degree, she could not contain herself, but shed a flood of tears, which she endeavored to conceal from me. While we were both in this deep affliction, I perceived a man enter the room, who in his person appeared to be as crooked and distorted as great S, and began to express himself in these terms, with a tone of voice as dismal and melancholy as those who exhort and pray with persons who are going to be executed: "Alas! poor Benvenuto, your work is spoiled, and the misfortune admits of no remedy."

No sooner had I heard the words uttered by this messenger of evil but I cried out so loud that my voice might be heard to the skies, and got out of bed. I began immediately to dress, and, giving plenty of kicks and cuffs to the maid-servants and the boy as they offered to help me on with my clothes, I complained bitterly in these terms: "O you envious and treacherous wretches, this is a piece of villainy contrived on purpose; but I swear by the living God that I will sift it to the bottom, and, before I die, give such proofs who I am as shall not fail to astonish the whole world." Having huddled on my clothes, I went, with a mind boding evil, to the shop, where I found all those whom I had left so alert, and in such high spirits, standing in the utmost confusion and astonishment. I thereupon addrest them thus: "Listen, all of you, to what I am going to say; and since you either would not or could not follow the method I pointed out, obey me now that I am present: my work is before us, and let none of you offer to oppose or contradict me, for such cases as this require activity, and not counsel." Hereupon one Alessandro Lastricati had the assurance to say to me, "Look you, Benvenuto, you have undertaken a work which our art can not compass, and which is not to be effected by human power."

Hearing these words, I turned round in such a passion, and seemed so bent on mischief that both he and all the rest unanimously cried out to me, "Give your orders, and we will all second you in whatever you command: we will assist you as long as we have breath in our bodies." These kind and affectionate words they uttered, as I firmly believe, in a persuasion that I was on the point of expiring. I went directly to examine the furnace, and saw all the metal in it concreted. I thereupon ordered two of the helpers to step over the way to Capretta, a butcher, for a load of young oak, which had been above a year drying, and been offered me by Maria Ginevra, wife to the said Capretta.

Upon his bringing me the first bundles of it, I began to fill the grate. This sort of oak makes a brisker fire than any other wood whatever; but the wood of elder-trees and pine-trees is used in casting artillery, because it makes a mild and gentle fire. As soon as the concreted metal felt the power of this violent fire, it began to brighten and glitter. In another quarter I made them hurry the tubes with all possible expedition, and sent some of them to the roof of the house, to take care of the fire, which through the great violence of the wind had acquired new force; and toward the garden I had caused some tables with pieces of tapestry and old clothes to be placed, in order to shelter me from the rain. As soon as I had applied the proper remedy to each evil, I with a loud voice cried out to my men to bestir themselves and lend a helping hand; so that when they saw that the concreted metal began to melt again, the whole body obeyed me with such zeal and alacrity that every man did the work of three.

Then I caused a mass of pewter weighing about sixty pounds to be thrown upon the metal in the furnace, which with the other helps, as the brisk wood fire, and stirring it, sometimes with iron, and sometimes with long poles, soon became completely dissolved. Finding that, contrary to the opinion of my ignorant assistants, I had effected what seemed as difficult as to raise the dead, I recovered my vigor to such a degree that I no longer perceived whether I had any fever, nor had I the least apprehension of death. Suddenly a loud noise was heard, and a glittering of fire flashed before our eyes, as if it had been the darting of a thunderbolt. Upon the appearance of this extraordinary phenomenon, terror seized on all present, and on none more than myself. This tremendous noise being over, we began to stare at each other, and perceived that the cover of the furnace had burst and flown off, so that the bronze began to run.

I immediately caused the mouths of my mold to be opened; but, finding that the metal did not run with its usual velocity, and apprehending that the cause of it was that the fusibility of the metal was injured by the violence of the fire, I ordered all my dishes and porringers, which were in number about two hundred, to be placed one by one before my tubes, and part of them to be thrown into the furnace; upon which all present perceived that my bronze was completely dissolved, and that my mold was filling: they now with joy and alacrity assisted and obeyed me. I, for my part, was sometimes in one place, sometimes in another, giving my directions and assisting my men, before whom I offered up this prayer: "O God, I address myself to Thee, who of Thy divine power didst rise from the dead and ascend in glory to heaven. I acknowledge in gratitude this mercy that my mold has been filled: I fall prostrate before Thee, and with my whole heart return thanks to Thy divine majesty." My prayer being over, I took a plate of meat which stood upon a little bench, and ate with a great appetite. I then drank with all my journeymen and assistants, and went joyful and in good health to bed; for there were still two hours of night; and I rested as well as if I had been troubled with no manner of disorder.

My good housekeeper, without my having given any orders, had provided a young capon for my dinner. When I arose, which was not till about noon, she accosted me in high spirits, and said, merrily, "Is this the man that thought himself dying? It is my firm belief that the cuffs and kicks which you gave us last night, when you were quite frantic and possest, frightened away your fever, which, apprehending lest you should fall upon it in the same manner, took to flight." So my whole poor family, having got over such panics and hardships, without delay procured earthen vessels to supply the place of the pewter dishes and porringers, and we all dined together very cheerfully: indeed, I do not remember having ever in my life eaten a meal with greater satisfaction or with a better appetite.

My mortal enemy, Pier Francesco Ricci, the duke's steward, was very eager to know how the affair had turned out; so that the two whom I suspected of being the cause of my metal's concreting in the manner above related told me that I was not a man, but rather a downright devil, for I had compassed that which was not in the power of art to effect; with many other surprizing things which would have been too much even for the infernal powers. As they greatly exaggerated what had passed, perhaps, with a view of excusing themselves, the steward wrote to the duke, who was then at Pisa, an account still more pompous and more replete with the marvelous than that which the workmen had given him.

Having left my work to cool during two days after it was cast, I began gradually to uncover it. I first of all found the Medusa's head, which had come out admirably by the assistance of the vents, as I had observed to the duke that the property of fire was to fly upward. I proceeded to uncover the rest, and found that the other head, I mean that of Perseus, was likewise come out perfectly well. This occasioned me still greater surprize, because, as it is seen in the statue, it is much lower than that of Medusa, the mouth of that figure being placed over the head and shoulders of Perseus. I found that where the head of Perseus ends, all the bronze was exhausted which I had in my furnace. This surprized me very much, that there should not be anything over and above what is necessary in casting. My astonishment, indeed, was raised to such a degree that I looked upon it as a miracle immediately wrought by the Almighty. I went on uncovering it, with great success, and found every part turn out to admiration, till I reached the foot of the right leg, which supports the figure, where I found the heel come out: so, proceeding to examine it, and thinking that the whole was filled up, in one respect I was glad, in another sorry, because I had told the duke it would not have that effect. Continuing, however, to uncover it, I found that not only the toes were wanting, but part of the foot itself, so that there was almost one-half deficient. This occasioned me some new trouble; but I was not displeased at it, because I could thereby convince the duke that I understood my business thoroughly; and tho there had come out a great deal more of that foot than I thought there would, the reason was that, in consequence of the several accidents that had happened, it was heated much more than it could have been in the regular course of business—especially as the pewter plates had been thrown into the furnace, a thing never done before.

GIORGIO VASARI

Born in Arrezo, Italy, in 1511, died in Florence in 1574; architect and painter as well as writer; many of his pictures produced in Florence and Rome; built a portion of the Uffizi Palace; only known in our day for his "Lives of Italian Architects, Painters, and Sculptors," published in 1550.

OF RAPHAEL AND HIS EARLY DEATH[1]

THE large and liberal hand wherewith heaven is sometimes pleased to accumulate the infinite riches of its treasures on the head of one sole favorite—showering on him all those rare gifts and graces which are more commonly distributed among a larger number of individuals, and accorded at long intervals of time only—has been clearly exemplified in the well-known instance of Raphael Sanzio of Urbino.

No less excellent than graceful, he was endowed by nature with all that modesty and goodness which may occasionally be perceived in those few favored persons who enhance the gracious sweetness of a disposition more than usually gentle, by the fair ornament of a winning amenity, always ready to conciliate and constantly giving evidence of the most refined consideration for

[1] From "The Lives of the Most Famous Painters, Sculptors and Architects," as translated by Mrs. Jonathan Foster. An earlier translation is the one by William Aglionby (1719).

all persons, and under every circumstance. The world received the gift of this artist from the hand of Nature, when, vanquished by Art in the person of Michelangelo, she deigned to be subjugated in that of Raphael, not by art only but by goodness also. And of a truth, since the greater number of artists had up to that period derived from nature a certain rudeness and eccentricity, which not only rendered them uncouth and fantastic, but often caused the shadows and darkness of vice to be more conspicuous in their lives than the light and splendor of those virtues by which man is rendered immortal—so was there good cause wherefore she should, on the contrary make all the rarest qualities of the heart to shine resplendently in her Raphael; perfecting them by so much diffidence, grace, application to study, and excellence of life, that these alone would have sufficed to veil or neutralize every fault, however important, and to efface all defects, however glaring they might have been. Truly may we affirm that those who are the possessors of endowments so rich and varied as were assembled in the person of Raphael, are scarcely to be called simple men only—they are rather, if it be permitted so to speak, entitled to the appellation of mortal gods; and further are we authorized to declare that he who by means of his works has left an honored name in the records of fame here below may also hope to enjoy such rewards in heaven as are commensurate to and worthy of their labors and merits.

Raphael was born at Urbino—a most renowned city of Italy—on Good Friday of the year 1483, at three o'clock of the night. His father was a certain Giovanni de' Santi; a painter of no great eminence in his art, but a man of sufficient intelligence nevertheless, and perfectly competent to direct his children into that good way which had not, for his misfortune, been laid open to himself in his younger days. And first, as he knew how important it is that a child should be nourished by the milk of its own mother, and not by that of the hired nurse, so he determined when his son Raphael (to whom he gave that name at his baptism, as being one of good augury) was born to him, that the mother[2] of the child, he having no other—as, indeed, he never had more—should herself be the nurse of the child. Giovanni further desired that in his tender years the boy should rather be brought up to the habits of his own family, and beneath his paternal roof, than be sent where he must acquire habits and manners less refined and modes of thought less commendable, in the houses of the peasantry or other untaught persons. As the child became older, Giovanni began to instruct him in the first principles of painting; perceiving that he was much inclined to that art, and finding him to be endowed with a most admirable genius; few years had passed, therefore, before Raphael, tho still but a child, became a valuable assistant to his father in the numerous works which the latter executed in the state of Urbino.

At length this good and affectionate father, knowing that his son would acquire but little of his art from himself, resolved to place him with Pietro Perugino, who, according to what Giovanni

[2] Raphael's mother was Magia Ciarla, who died when he was eight years old. He was brought up by a stepmother.

had been told, was then considered to hold the first place among the painters of the time. Wherefore, proceeding to Perugia for that purpose, and finding Pietro to be absent from the city, he occupied himself—to the end that he might await the return of the master with the less inconvenience—in the execution of certain works for the church of San Francesco in that place. But when Pietro had returned to Perugia, Giovanni, who was a person of very good manners and pleasing deportment, soon formed an amicable acquaintanceship with him; and when the proper opportunity arrived, made known to him the desire he had conceived, in the most suitable manner that he could devise. Thereupon Pietro, who was also exceedingly courteous, as well as a lover of fine genius, agreed to accept the care of Raphael. Giovanni then returned to Urbino; and having taken the boy, tho not without many tears from his mother, who loved him tenderly, he conducted him to Perugia: when Pietro no sooner beheld his manner of drawing, and observed the pleasing deportment of the youth than he conceived that opinion of him which was in due time so amply confirmed by the results produced in the after life of Raphael. . . .

But I have now discoursed respecting these questions of art at more length perhaps than was needful, and will return to the life and death of Raphael. This master lived in the strictest intimacy with Bernardo Divizio, Cardinal of Bibbiena, who had for many years importuned him to take a wife of his selection; nor had Raphael directly refused compliance with the wishes of the cardinal, but had put the matter off, by saying that he would wait some three or four years longer. The term which he had thus set approached before Raphael had thought of it, when he was reminded by the cardinal of his promise; and being as he ever was just and upright, he would not depart from his word, and therefore accepted a niece of the cardinal himself for his wife. But as this engagement was nevertheless a very heavy restraint to him, he put off the marriage from time to time; insomuch that several months passed, and the ceremony had not yet taken place.[3] Yet this was not done without a very honorable motive; for Raphael having been for many years in the service of the count, and being the creditor of Leo X for a large sum of money, had received an intimation to the effect that when the hall with which he was then occupied was completed, the pontiff intended to reward him for his labors as well as to do honor to his talents by bestowing on him the red hat, of which he meant to distribute a considerable number, many of them being designed for persons whose merits were greatly inferior to those of Raphael.

The painter meanwhile did not abandon the light attachment by which he was enchained: and one day, on returning to his house from one of these secret visits, he was seized with a violent

---

[3] The lady here referred to was Maria Bibiena, who is now believed to have died before Raphael. To her, by testamentary injunction from Raphael, an inscription was afterward set up in the Pantheon, where Raphael himself was buried. In 1833 Raphael's tomb was opened, the skeleton being found with the skull showing scarcely any decay of the bony parts.

fever,⁴ which being mistaken for a cold, the physicians inconsiderately caused him to be bled; whereby he found himself exhausted, when he had rather required to be strengthened. Thereupon he made his will, and as a good Christian he sent the object of his attachment from the house, but left her a sufficient provision wherewith she might live in decency: having done so much, he divided his property among his disciples,—Giulio Romano, that is to say, whom he always loved greatly, and Giovanni Francesco, with whom was joined a certain priest of Urbino who was his kinsman, but whose name I do not know. He furthermore commanded that a certain portion of his property should be employed in the restoration of one of the ancient tabernacles in Santa Maria Ritonda,⁵ which he had selected as his burial-place, and for which he had ordered that an altar, with the figure of Our Lady in marble, should be prepared; all that he possest besides he bequeathed to Giulio Romano and Giovanni Francesco,—naming Messer Baldassare da Pescia, who was then datary to the Pope, as his executor. He then confest, and in much contrition completed the course of his life, on the day whereon it had commenced, which was Good Friday. The master was then in the thirty-seventh year of his age, and as he embellished the world by his talents while on earth, so is it to be believed that his soul is now adorning heaven.

After his death, the body of Raphael was placed

---

⁴ Raphael is believed to have contracted this fever while engaged in searching for antiquities in Roman localities where fever might easily be contracted.

⁵ The Pantheon.

at the upper end of the hall wherein he had last worked, with the picture of the Transfiguration which he had executed for Cardinal Ginlio de' Medici at the head of the corpse. He who, regarding that living picture, afterward turned to consider that dead body, felt his heart bursting with grief as he beheld them. The loss of Raphael caused the cardinal to command that this work should be placed on the high altar of San Pietro da Montorio, where it has ever since been held in the utmost veneration for its own great value, as well as for the excellence of its author. The remains of this divine artist received that honorable sepulture which the noble spirit whereby they had been informed had so well deserved; nor was there any artist in Rome who did not deeply bewail the loss sustained by the departure of the master, or who failed to accompany his remains to their repose.

The death of Raphael was in like manner deplored by all the papal court: not only because he had formed part thereof, since he had held the office of chamberlain to the pontiff, but also because Leo X had esteemed him so highly, that his loss occasioned that sovereign the bitterest grief. O most happy and thrice blest spirit, of whom all are proud to speak, whose actions are celebrated with praise by all men, and the least of whose works left behind thee is admired and prized!

When this noble artist died, well might Painting have departed also; for when he closed his eyes, she too was left as it were blind. But now to us, whose lot it is to come after him, there remains to imitate the good, or rather the excellent, of which he has left us the example; and as our obligations to him and his great merits well deserve, to retain the most grateful remembrance of him in our hearts, while we ever maintain his memory in the highest honor with our lips. To him of a truth it is that we owe the possession of invention, coloring, and execution, brought alike and altogether to that point of perfection for which few could have dared to hope; nor has any man ever aspired to pass before him.

And in addition to the benefits which this great master conferred on art, being as he was its best friend, we have the further obligation to him of having taught us by his life in what manner we should comport ourselves toward great men, as well as toward those of lower degree, and even toward the lowest; nay, there was among his many extraordinary gifts one of such value and importance, that I can never sufficiently admire it, and always think thereof with astonishment. This was the power accorded to him by heaven, of bringing all who approached his presence into harmony; an effect inconceivably surprizing in our calling, and contrary to the nature of our artists; yet all, I do not say of the inferior grades only, but even those who lay claim to be great personages (and of this humor our art produces immense numbers), became as of one mind, once they began to labor in the society of Raphael; continuing in such unity and concord that all harsh feelings and evil dispositions became subdued, and disappeared at the sight of him, every vile and base thought departing from the mind before his influence. Such harmony prevailed at no other time than his own.

JACQUES CASANOVA
CHEVALIER DE SEINGALT

Born in Venice in 1725, died probably in 1803; his father an actor, his mother a shoemaker's daughter; educated for the priesthood; expelled in disgrace from the seminary; entered the Venetian military service, and began a career of intrigue and adventure as chronicled in his memoirs; wandered to almost every quarter of Europe, living by his wits as journalist, doctor, mesmerist, and diplomat; effected an entrance to many high social circles and was presented to Catharine of Russia, Louis XV, Frederick the Great, Rousseau, Voltaire, and Madame de Pompadour; arrested in Venice as a spy in 1755, imprisoned and escaped; afterward honored by Italian princes and decorated by the Pope; became librarian to Count Waldstein in Bohemia in his fifty-seventh year; his "Memoirs" notable as a picture of manners and morals at their worst, chronicled with the utmost frankness.

HIS INTERVIEW WITH FREDERICK THE GREAT [1]

At that time I am writing of, Lord Keith was living in Berlin, resting on his laurels, beloved and cherished by the king, but taking no active part in politics, as he was over eighty years of age, but simple and charming as ever. He received me kindly, and exprest a hope that I should remain some time in Berlin, as he knew, to a certain extent, the vicissitudes of my past life. I replied that I would gladly settle there if the king would give me a suitable appointment; but

[1] From the abridged edition of the "Memoirs," published in London in 1902, the translator being anonymous.

when I asked him to speak to the king for me, he replied that that would do more harm than good. "His majesty piques himself on knowing men better than any one else. He likes to judge them himself; sometimes he discovers merit when no one else sees any, and sometimes vice versa."

He advised me to write to the king and beg an interview.

"When you speak to him, you can say that you know me, and he will then probably ask me about you; you may be sure that I shall say nothing but what is to your credit."

"I, my lord, write to a king to whom I have no introduction? I could not think of it."

"But you wish to speak to him, do you not?"

"Certainly."

"That is enough; your letter need contain nothing but the expression of your desire."

"Will the king answer me?"

"Without doubt, for he answers everybody. He will tell you when it will please him to receive you. Take my advice, and let me know how you get on."

I did as he suggested, and wrote a simple and respectful letter, asking when and where I might present myself to his majesty. The day but one after I received a reply signed Frederick, acknowledging the receipt of my letter, and saying I should find him at four o'clock that day in the gardens at Sans Souci.

As my readers may imagine, I was delighted at having obtained a rendezvous, and arrived at the palace an hour before the appointed time very simply drest in black. I entered the courtyard, and as I did not see any one, not even a sentinel,

I went up a short staircase, and opening a door, found myself in a picture-gallery. A guardian came up and offered to show me the collection.

"I did not come here to admire these works of art," I said, "but to speak to the king, who told me he would be in the garden."

"At this moment he is at his concert, playing the flute. 'Tis his dessert after dinner, and he treats himself to it every day. Did he fix any hour?"

"Yes, four o'clock, but he may have forgotten."

"He never forgets. He will be punctual, and you had better wait in the garden."

I had not been there long, when I saw him approaching. The king followed by his secretary and a fine spaniel. As soon as he saw me he pronounced my name, at the same time taking off his bad old hat; he then asked, in a terrible voice, what I wanted.

I stood looking at him in silence.

"Well, can't you speak? Isn't it you who wrote to me?"

"Yes, sire; but now I can't remember what I had to say. I did not think the majesty of a king could so dazzle my senses. I shall be better prepared in future. My lord marshal ought to have warned me."

"Ah! he knows you, does he? Come, let us walk about. What did you wish to say? What do you think of this garden?"

He ordered me to speak of his garden! I should have said I knew nothing of gardens to any one else, but if he chose to think me a connoisseur I must fain pretend to be one. At the risk of exposing my ignorance, I replied that it was superb.

"But," he said, "the gardens at Versailles are far finer."

"I own it, sire; but that is because of the fountains."

"True; but it is not my fault. There is no water here. I have spent more than three hundred thousand crowns, but without success."

"Three hundred thousand crowns, sire! If your majesty spent that sum, there should have been abundance of water."

"Ah! ah! I see you are a hydraulic architect."

Could I tell him he was mistaken? I was afraid of displeasing him, so I simply bent my head. This could be taken for yes or no. Thank God, he did not continue to talk on this subject, or I should have been terribly put to it, for I did not know the very rudiments of hydraulics.

Still walking up and down, and turning his head right and left, he asked me what the Venetian forces, naval and military, amounted to. Now I was on my own ground. "Twenty men of war, sire, and a large number of galleys."

"And what land forces?"

"Seventy thousand men, sire, all subjects of the republic, and counting all that, only one man from each village."

"That is not true. I suppose you want to amuse me with your fables. You must be a financier; tell me, what do you think of the taxes?"

This was the first interview I had ever had with royalty. Considering his style, his abrupt change of subject, and his sudden digressions, I felt as tho I had been called on to act in one of those improvised Italian comedies in which, if the actor stops short for a word, the pit and the gallery hiss him mercilessly. I immediately assumed the style of a financier, and replied that I was acquainted with the theory of taxation.

"That is what I want," he replied, "for the practise does not concern you."

"There are three kinds of taxes, taking into consideration their effects: one is ruinous, one is unfortunately necessary, and the third is always excellent."

"That is good; go on."

"The ruinous tax is the royal tax; the necessary one is the military one; and the excellent one is the popular tax."

I wanted to throw him off his beat a little, as I had not got up my subject.

"The royal tax, sire, is the one which empties the purses of the subjects to swell the coffers of the sovereign."

"And that is the ruinous one, you say?"

"Always, sire, for it stops the circulation of money, which is the soul of commerce and the backbone of the state."

"Yet, you consider the army tax necessary?"

"Unfortunately necessary, for war is a dire calamity."

"Perhaps. And how about the popular tax?"

"It is always excellent, for what the king takes from his people with one hand, he gives them back with the other, turning it into useful channels, protecting science and art, and so contributing to the general social well-being; in fact, the king adds to general happiness by employing the money drawn from the taxes as his wisdom dictates.''

"There is a good deal of truth in what you say. No doubt you know Calsabigi?''

"I ought to know him, sire, for we established the Genoese lottery in Paris together, seven years ago.''

"And under what head would you class that tax, if you admit it to be one?''

"It is one, sire, and not one of the least important. It is a good tax, if the king spends the profits in a useful manner.''

"But supposing he loses?''

"One chance in fifty, sire.''

"Is that the result of an exact calculation?''

"As exact, sire, as all political calculations.''

"They are often wrong.''

"They are never wrong, sire, if God remains neutral.''

"Why drag the Deity into such a question?''

"Let us say then, sire, luck, or destiny.''

"That is better. Perhaps I agree with you about the moral calculations, but I do not like your Genoese lottery. It seems to me a mere swindle, and I would not have anything to do with it, even if I were certain to win always.''

"Your majesty is right, for the public would never support lotteries were they not led away by false security.''

Then he tried one or two other points, but I met him without flinching. Suddenly he stopt short and looked me over from head to foot.

"Do you know that you are a very handsome man?''

"Is it possible, sire, that after a long scientific

205

dissertation, your majesty can credit me with merely the qualities which distinguish your majesty's grenadiers?"

The king smiled with kind malice, then said: "As it seems that Lord Keith knows you, I will speak to him about you."

He then took off his hat again, for he was never chary of his bows, and I, making him a profound reverence, withdrew.

Three or four days after the lord marshal told me the king was very pleased with me, and had said he would try and find me something to do.

OTHER COUNTRIES

1465—1909

DESIDERIUS ERASMUS

Born in Rotterdam in 1465, died in Switzerland in 1536; an illegitimate son, left an orphan at thirteen and deprived of his inheritance by guardians, who compelled him to enter a monastery; entered in 1491 the services of the Bishop of Cambray, who enabled him to study at the University of Paris; visited England in 1498-99, and again in 1510-14; settled at Basel in 1521; removed to Freiburg in 1529; refused offers of ecclesiastical preferment; endeavored to reform the Church without dismembering it; at first favored, but afterward opposed Luther; published a Latin translation of the New Testament in 1516.

SPECIMENS OF HIS WIT AND WISDOM [1]

OF all birds, the eagle alone has seemed to wise men the apt type of royalty: not beautiful, not musical, not fit for food; but carnivorous, greedy, plundering, destroying, combating, solitary, hateful to all, the curse of all, and with its

[1] Some of these passages are from Crowther's translation of the "Enchiridion"; others from Bishop Kennett's translation of "The Praise of Folly"; Sir Roger L'Estrange's translation of the "Colloquies"; and Froude's translation of the "Letters," as given in his "Life of Erasmus." English translations from Erasmus began to be made soon after the appearance of his works in the original. In 1522 appeared "A Lyttel Booke of good Maners for Chyldren, as translated into the vulgare Englysshe tonge, by Robert Whytynton, laureate poete." It was printed by Wykyns de Worde. In 1533 the "Enchiridion" was translated by Will Tindal and printed by Wykyns de Worde. In 1542 appeared "Apothegms," translated by Nicholas Udall. In 1567 "The Praise of Folie" was "Englisshed" by Sir Thomas Chalones. In 1671 appeared the "Colloquies," translated by "H. M.," and in 1720 "Proverbs" gathered out of Erasmus.

great powers of doing harm, surpassing them in its desire of doing it.

Princes must be endured, lest tyranny should give way to anarchy, a still greater evil. This has been demonstrated by the experience of many states; and lately the insurrection of the German Boers has taught us that the cruelty of princes is better to be borne than the universal confusion of anarchy.

There is a wretched class of men, of low degree, yet full of malice; not less dingy, nor less filthy, nor less vile than beetles; who nevertheless by a certain obstinate malignity of disposition, tho they can never do good to any mortal, become frequently troublesome to the great. They frighten by their ugliness, they molest by their noise, they offend by their stench; they buzz round us, they cling to us, they lie in ambush for us, so that it is often better to be at enmity with powerful men than to attack these beetles; whom it is a disgrace even to overcome, and whom no one can either shake off or encounter without some pollution.[2]

The generality of mankind place religion in ceremonies or creeds; a certain appointment of psalms, or in bodily exercises. If you examine them about spiritual matters, you will find them merely carnal.

God despised the burnt-offerings, new moons and Sabbaths, the calling of assemblies, and the appointed feasts of His people, while they were evil-doers, altho He Himself had commanded them; and will any man dare to compare his own paltry institutions with the divine precepts? You may

[2] Erasmus here refers to mendicant friars.

read in Isaiah what contempt and loathing he expresses concerning them. When He speaks of rites, ceremonies, and the multitude of prayers, does He not, as it were, point at those men who measure religion by psalms, prayers, creeds, or other human institutions?

Christ is nothing else than love, simplicity, patience, purity,—in short, all that He himself is; and the devil is nothing but that which draws us away from these ideals.

What shall I say of such as cry up and maintain the cheat of pardons and indulgences? that by these compute the time of each soul's residence in purgatory, and assign them a longer or shorter continuance according as they purchase more or fewer of these paltry pardons? By this easy way of purchasing pardons, any notorious highwayman, any plundering soldier, any bribe-taking judge, shall disburse some part of his unjust gains and so think all his grossest impieties atoned for. So many perjuries, lusts, drunkennesses, quarrels, bloodsheds, cheats, treacheries, debaucheries, shall all be, as it were, struck a bargain for; and such a contract made as if they had paid off all arrears and might now begin a new score.

Among these some make a good profitable trade of beggary, going abroad from house to house, not like the apostles to break their bread, but to beg it; nay, thrust themselves into all public houses, crowd into passage boats, get into travelers' wagons, and omit no chance of craving people's charity, and injuring common beggars by interloping in their traffic of alms.

Some were spewing, some were praying. I remember one Englishman there. What mountains of gold did he promise to our Lady of Walsingham if he ever got safe ashore again! One made a vow to deposit a relic of the Cross in this place; another to put a relic of it in that;—some promised to turn monks; one vowed a pilgrimage, barefooted and bareheaded, in a coat of mail, and begging his bread all the way, to St. James of Compostella. I could not but laugh at one fellow there. He vowed as loud as he could bellow to the St. Christopher in the great church at Paris (that the saint might be sure to hear him) a wax candle as big as the saint himself. Now, you must know that the Paris St. Christopher is enormous, and rather a mountain than a statue. He was so loud, and went over and over with it so often, that a friend of his gave him a touch on the elbow: "Take care what you promise," said he; "if you should sell yourself, you could not buy such a candle." "Hold your tongue, you fool," says the other (softly, so that St. Christopher might not hear). "Let me but set foot on land once more, and St. Christopher has good luck if he get even a tallow candle from me."

I had rather lose all Duns Scotus, and twenty more such as he, than one Cicero or Plutarch. Not that I am wholly against them, either: but from the reading of the one I find myself to become honester and better; whereas I rise from the other extremely dull, indifferent to virtue, but violently bent on cavil and contention.

Read first the best books. The important thing for you is not how much you know, but the quality of what you know. Divide your day and give to each part of it a special occupation. Never work at night. It dulls the brain and hurts the health.

I would not change my freedom for the best bishopric in the world.

I am now fifty-one years old. I am not enamored of life, but it is worth while to continue a little longer with such a prospect of a golden age. All looks brighter now. I myself, insignificant I, have contributed something. I have at least stirred the bile of those who would not have the world grow wiser, and only fools now snarl at me. One of them said in a sermon lately, in a lamentable voice, that all was now over with the Christian faith.

Old institutions can not be rooted up in an instant. Quiet argument may do more than wholesale condemnation. Avoid all appearance of sedition. Keep cool. Do not get angry. Do not hate anybody. Do not get excited over the noise which you have made. May Christ give you His spirit, for His own glory and the world's good.[3]

The world is waking out of a long deep sleep. The old ignorance is still defended with tooth and claw, but we have kings and nobles now on our side.

For yourself, the intelligence of your country will preserve the memories of your virtues, and scholars will tell how a king once reigned there who in his own person revived the virtues of the ancient heroes.[4]

The justest war can hardly approve itself to any reasonable person. The people build cities,

---

[3] This paragraph is from a letter to Luther.
[4] From a letter to Henry VIII of England.

the princes destroy them, and even victory brings more ill than good.

My work has been to restore a buried literature, and recall divines from their hair-splittings to a knowledge of the New Testament.

Do not mistake me. Theology itself I reverence and always have reverenced. I am speaking merely of the theologasters of our own time, whose brains are the rottenest, intellects the dullest, doctrines the thorniest, manners the brutalest, life the foulest, speech the spitefulest, hearts the blackest, that I have ever encountered in the world.

You say that I can not die better than among my brethren. I am not so sure of that. Your religion is in your dress; your religious orders, as you call them, have done the Church small service.

What a thing it is to cultivate literature! Better far to grow cabbages. Bishops have thanked me for my work, the Pope has thanked me; but these tyrants, the mendicant friars, never leave me alone with their railing.[5]

I wish there could be an end of scholastic subtleties, and Christ be taught plainly and simply. The reading of the Bible and the early Fathers will have this effect.

Wrangling about the nature of the Second Person of the Trinity, as if Christ were a malignant demon, ready to destroy you if you made a mistake about His nature! Reduce the articles of faith to the fewest and simplest. Let our divines show their faith by their works, and convert Turks by the beauty of their lives.

May not a man be a Christian, who can not ex-

[5] From a letter to Cardinal Wolsey.

plain philosophically how the nativity of the Son differs from the procession of the Holy Spirit? The sum of religion is peace, which can only be when definitions are as few as possible, and opinion is left free on many subjects. Our present problems are said to be waiting for the next Ecumenical Council. Better let them wait till the veil is removed, and we see God face to face.

Luther's party have urged me to join them, and Luther's enemies have done their best to drive me to it by their furious attacks on me in their sermons. Neither have succeeded. Christ I know; Luther I know not. I have said nothing, except that Luther ought to be answered and not crusht. We must bear almost anything rather than throw the world into confusion. The actual facts of things are not to be blurted out at all times and places, and in all companies. I was the first to oppose the publication of Luther's books. I recommended Luther himself to publish nothing revolutionary. I feared always that revolution would be the end, and I would have done more had I not been afraid that I might be found fighting against the Spirit of God.

As to Luther himself, I perceived that the better a man was, the less he was Luther's enemy. Can it be right to persecute a man of unblemished life, in whose writings distinguished and excellent persons have found so much to admire? The Pope has no worse enemies than his foolish defenders. He can crush any man if he pleases, but empires based only on terror do not last.

By burning Luther's books you may rid your book-shelves of him, but you will not rid men's minds of him.

Curses and threats may beat the fire down for the moment, but it will burst out worse than ever. The Bull has lost Luther no friends, and gained none for the Pope.

All admit that the corruptions of the Church required a drastic medicine. But drugs wrongly given make the sick man worse. I said this to the King of Denmark lately. He laughed, and answered that small dose would be of no use; that the whole system needed purging. For myself, I am a man of peace and hate quarrels.

It is easy to call Luther "a fungus"; it is not easy to answer him.

They may chain the tongues of men; they can not touch their minds.

They call me a Lutheran. Had I but held out a little finger to Luther, Germany would have seen what I could do. But I would rather die ten times over than make a schism.

I do not object generally to the evangelical doctrines, but there is much in Luther's teachings which I dislike. He runs everything which he touches into extravagance. Do not fear that I shall oppose evangelical truth. I left many faults in him unnoticed, lest I should injure the gospel. I hope mankind will be the better for the acrid medicines with which he has dosed them. Perhaps we needed a surgeon who would use knife and cautery.[6]

Your Holiness[7] requires my advice, and you wish to see me. I would go to you with pleasure if my health allowed. But the road over the Alps is long. The lodgings on the way are dirty and

[6] From a letter to Melanchthon.

[7] From a letter to Adrian VI, who became Pope in 1522

inconvenient. The smell from the stoves is intolerable. The wine is sour and disagrees with me. As to writing against Luther, I have not learning enough. One party says I agree with Luther because I do not oppose him. The other finds fault with me because I do oppose him. I did what I could. I advised him to be moderate, and I only made his friends my enemies. They quote this and that to show we are alike. I could find a hundred passages where St. Paul seems to teach the doctrines which they condemn in Luther. I did not anticipate what a time was coming. I did, I admit, help to bring it on; but I was always willing to submit what I wrote to the Church. Those counsel you best who advise gentle measures. Your Holiness wishes to set things right, and you say to me, "Come to Rome. Write a book against Luther. Declare war against his party." Come to Rome? Tell a crab to fly. The crab will say, "Give me wings." I say, "Give me back my youth and strength." If I write anything at Rome, it will be thought that I am bribed. If I write temperately, I shall seem trifling. If I copy Luther's style, I shall stir a hornets' nest.

MIGUEL DE CERVANTES

Born in 1547, died in 1616; of a poor but noble family; studied at Salamanca; served as a chamberlain to the future Cardinal Aquaviva in Rome in 1570; in the army under Don John of Austria against the Turks; lost the use of his left arm in the Battle of Lepanto in 1571; taken prisoner and spent five years in slavery in Algiers, being ransomed in 1580; returned to Spain and married in 1584; imprisoned for debt and served as an amanuensis; wrote the first part of "Don Quixote" at Valladolid in 1603; returned to Madrid and published the second part in 1615; his other works are "Galatea," published in 1584, "Moral Tales" in 1613, "Journey to Parnassus" in 1614, and twenty or more plays.

I

THE BEGINNINGS OF DON QUIXOTE'S CAREER [1]

In a village of La Mancha, the name of which I have no desire to call to mind, there lived not long since one of those gentlemen that keep a lance in the lance-rack, and an old buckler, a lean

[1] The first translation of "Don Quixote" into any language was the one begun into English by Thomas Shelton in 1607, only two years after the publication of the original Spanish. It was followed in 1687 by a translation by John Philips, a nephew of Milton. Peter A. Motteux, who had previously completed the standard translation of Rabelais begun by Urquhart, published a version of "Don Quixote" in 1719, which was afterward reissued by John Gibson Lockhart with notes by himself. Charles Jarvis, a painter, who was a friend of Pope, published a translation in 1742. This was followed in 1755 by a translation

218

hack, and a greyhound for coursing. An olla of rather more beef than mutton, a salad on most nights, scraps on Saturdays, lentils on Fridays, and a pigeon or so extra on Sundays, made away with three-quarters of his income. The rest of it went in a doublet of fine cloth and velvet breeches and shoes to match for holidays, while on week-days he made a brave figure in his best homespun. He had in his house a housekeeper past forty, a niece under twenty, and a lad for the field and market-place, who used to saddle the hack as well as handle the bill-hook. The age of this gentleman of ours was bordering on fifty; he was of a hardy habit, spare, gaunt-featured, a very early riser and a great sportsman. They will have it his surname was Quixada or Quesada (for here there is some difference of opinion among the authors who write on the subject), altho from reasonable conjectures it seems plain that he called himself Quixana. This, however, is of but little importance to our tale; it will be enough not to stray a hair's-breadth from the truth in the telling of it.

You must know then that the above-named gentleman, whenever he was at leisure (which was mostly all the year round) gave himself up

by Tobias Smollet, which seems to have been made from the French rather than the Spanish. In 1818 a sister of R. Smirke brought out another version. Still another by A. J. Duffield was issued in 1851 and another by John Ormsby in 1885. The translation by John Jarvis has probably had the greatest vogue. The passages given in this collection are from his version. H. E. Watts, author of a notable recent "Life of Cervantes," published also a translation of "Don Quixote," which has been thought to surpass others.

to reading books of chivalry with such ardor and avidity that he almost entirely neglected the pursuit of his field-sports, and even the management of his property; and to such a pitch did his eagerness and infatuation go that he sold many an acre of tillage-land to buy books of chivalry to read, and brought home as many of them as he could get. But of all there were none he liked so well as those of the famous Feliciano de Silva's compositions, for their lucidity of style and complicated conceits were as pearls in his sight, particularly when in his reading he came upon courtships and cartels, where he often found passages like: "The reason of the unreason with which my reason is afflicted, so weakens my reason that with reason I murmur at your beauty"; or again: "The high heavens, that of your divinity divinely fortify you with the stars, render you deserving of the desert your greatness deserves." Over conceits of this sort the poor gentleman lost his wits, and used to lie awake striving to understand them and worm the meaning out of them; what Aristotle himself could not have made out or extracted, had he come to life again for that special purpose. He was not at all easy about the wounds which Don Belianis gave and took, because it seemed to him that, great as were the surgeons who had cured him, he must have had his face and body covered all over with seams and scars. He commended, however, the author's way of ending his book with the promise of that interminable adventure; and many a time was he tempted to take up his pen and finish it properly as is there proposed, which no doubt he would have done, and made a successful piece of work of it too, had not greater and more absorbing thoughts prevented him.

Many an argument did he have with the curate of his village (a learned man, and a graduate of Siguenza), as to which had been the better knight, Palmerin of England or Amadis of Gaul. Master Nicholas, the village barber, however, used to say that neither of them came up to the Knight of Phœbus, and that if there was any could compare with *him* it was Don Galaor, the brother of Amadis of Gaul, because he had a spirit that was equal to every occasion, and was no finikin knight, nor lachrymose like his brother, while in the matter of valor he was not a whit behind him. In short, he became so absorbed in his books that he spent his nights from sunset to sunrise, and his days from dawn to dark, poring over them; and what with little sleep and much reading his brains got so dry that he lost his wits. His fancy grew full of what he used to read about in his books—enchantments, quarrels, battles, challenges, wounds, wooings, loves, agonies and all sorts of impossible nonsense; and it so possest his mind that the whole fabric of invention and fancy he read of was true, that to him no history in the world had more reality in it. He used to say the Cid Ruy Diaz was a very good knight, but that he was not to be compared with the Knight of the Burning Sword, who with one back-stroke cut in half two fierce and monstrous giants. He thought more of Bernardo del Carpio because at Roncesvalles he slew Roland in spite of enchantments, availing himself of the artifice of Hercules when he strangled Antæus the son of Terra in his arms. He ap-

proved highly of the giant Morgante, because
altho of the giant breed, which is always arrogant and ill-conditioned, he alone was affable and
well bred. But above all he admired Reinaldos
of Montalban; especially when he saw him sally-
ing forth from his castle and robbing every one he
met, and when beyond the seas he stole that
image of Mohammed which, as history says, was
entirely of gold. And to have a bout of kicking
at that traitor of a Ganelon he would have given
his housekeeper, and his niece into the bargain.

In short, his wits were quite gone, he hit upon
the strangest notion that ever madman in this
world hit upon: and that was that he fancied
it was right and requisite, as well for the support
of his own honor as for the service of his country,
that he should make a knight-errant of himself,
roaming the world over in full armor and on
horseback in quest of adventures, and putting in
practise himself all that he had read of as being
the usual practises of knights-errant; righting
every kind of wrong, and exposing himself to
peril and danger from which, in the issue, he was
to reap eternal renown and fame. Already the
poor man saw himself crowned, by the might of
his arm, Emperor of Trebizond at least; and so,
led away by the intense enjoyment he found in
these pleasant fancies, he set himself forthwith
to put his scheme into execution.

The first thing he did was to clean up some
armor that had belonged to his great-grandfather,
and had been for ages lying forgotten in a corner,
eaten with rust and covered with mildew. He
scoured and polished it as best he could, but he
perceived one great defect in it; that it had no

closed helmet, nothing but a simple morion. This deficiency, however, his ingenuity supplied, for he contrived a kind of half-helmet of pasteboard which, fitted on to the morion, looked like a whole one. It is true that in order to see if it was strong and fit to stand a cut he drew his sword and gave it a couple of slashes, the first of which undid in an instant what had taken him a week to do. The ease with which he had knocked it to pieces disconcerted him somewhat, and to guard against that danger he set to work again, fixing bars of iron on the inside until he was satisfied with its strength; and then, not caring to try any more experiments with it, he passed it and adopted it as a helmet of the most perfect construction.

He next proceeded to inspect his hack, which with more quartos than a real and more blemishes than the steed of Gonela, that *"tantum pellis et ossa fuit"* surpassed in his eyes the Bucephalus of Alexander or the Babieca of the Cid. Four days were spent in thinking what name to give him; because (as he said to himself) it was not right that a horse belonging to a knight so famous, and one with such merits of his own, should be without some distinctive name, and he strove to adapt it so as to indicate what he had been before belonging to a knight-errant, and what he then was; for it was only reasonable that, his master taking a new character, he should take a new name, and that it should be a distinguished and full-sounding one, befitting the new order and calling he was about to follow.

II

OF HOW DON QUIXOTE DIED[2]

As nothing that is man's can last forever, but all tends ever downward from its beginning to its end, and above all, man's life; and as Don Quixote's enjoyed no special dispensation from Heaven to stay its course,—its end and close came when he least looked for it. For—whether it was of the dejection the thought of his defeat produced, or of Heaven's will that so ordered it —a fever settled upon him and kept him in his bed for six days, during which he was often visited by his friends the curate, the bachelor, and the barber, while his good squire Sancho Panza never quitted his bedside. They, persuaded that it was grief at finding himself vanquished, and the object of his heart, the liberation and disenchantment of Dulcinea, unattained, that kept him in this state, strove by all the means in their power to cheer him up: the bachelor bidding him take heart and get up to begin his pastoral life; for which he himself, he said, had already composed an eclogue that would take the shine out of all Sannazaro[3] had ever written, and had bought with his own money two famous dogs to guard the flock, one called Barcino and the other Butron, which a herdsman of Quintanar had sold him.

[2] From "Don Quixote." Translated by John Jarvis.
[3] Jacopo Sannazaro was a Neapolitan poet, who wrote a work called "Arcadia."

But for all this Don Quixote could not shake off his sadness. His friends called in the doctor, who felt his pulse and was not very well satisfied with it, and said that in any case it would be well for him to attend to the health of his soul, as that of his body was in a bad way. Don Quixote heard this calmly; but not so his housekeeper, his niece, and his squire, who fell weeping bitterly, as if they had him lying dead before them. The doctor's opinion was that melancholy and depression were bringing him to his end. Don Quixote begged them to leave him to himself, as he had a wish to sleep a little. They obeyed, and he slept at one stretch, as the saying is, more than six hours, so that the housekeeper and niece thought he was going to sleep forever. But at the end of that time he woke up, and in a loud voice exclaimed, "Blest be Almighty God, who has shown me such goodness! In truth His mercies are boundless, and the sins of men can neither limit them nor keep them back!" . . .

They looked at one another, wondering at Don Quixote's words; but, tho uncertain, they were inclined to believe him, and one of the signs by which they came to the conclusion he was dying was this so sudden and complete return to his senses after having been mad; for to the words already quoted he added much more, so well exprest, so devout, and so rational, as to banish all doubt and convince them that he was sound of mind. The curate turned them all out, and, left alone with him, confest him. The bachelor went for the notary, and returned shortly afterward with him and with Sancho, who, having already learned from the bachelor the condition his master was in, and finding the housekeeper and niece weeping, began to blubber and shed tears.

The confession over, the curate came out saying: "Alonso Quixano the Good is indeed dying, and is indeed in his right mind; we may now go in to him, while he makes his will."

This news gave a tremendous impulse to the brimming eyes of the housekeeper, niece, and Sancho Panza his good squire, making the tears burst from their eyes and a host of sighs from their hearts; for, of a truth, as has been said more than once, whether as plain Alonso Quixano the Good, or as Don Quixote of La Mancha, Don Quixote was always of a gentle disposition and kindly in all his ways, and hence he was beloved not only by those of his own house, but by all who knew him.

The notary came in with the rest, and as soon as the preamble of the will had been set out and Don Quixote had commended his soul to God with all the devout formalities that are usual, coming to the bequests, he said: "*Item:* It is my will that, touching certain moneys in the hands of Sancho Panza (whom in my madness I made my squire), inasmuch as between him and me there have been certain accounts and debits and credits, no claim be made against him, nor any account demanded of him in respect of them; but that if anything remain over and above, after he has paid himself what I owe him, the balance, which will be but little, shall be his, and much good may it do him; and if as when I was mad I had a share in giving him the government of an island, so now that I am in my senses could I give him that cf a kingdom, it should be his, for the simplicity of his character and the fidelity of his conduct deserve it.'' And then, turning to Sancho, he said, ''Forgive me, my friend, that I led thee to seem as mad as myself, making thee fall into the same error I myself fell into, that there were and still are knights-errant in the world.''

''Ah!'' said Sancho weeping; ''don't die, master, but take my advice and live many years; for the foolishest thing a man can do in this life is to let himself die without rime or reason, without anybody killing him, or any hands but melancholy's making an end of him. Come, don't be lazy, but get up from your bed and let us take to the fields in shepherd's trim as we agreed. Perhaps behind some bush we shall find the lady Dulcinea disenchanted, as fine as fine can be. If it be that you are dying of vexation at having been vanquished, lay the blame on me, and say you were overthrown because I had girted Rosinante badly; besides, you must have seen in your books of chivalry that it is a common thing for knights to upset one another, and for him who is conquered to-day to be conqueror to-morrow.''

''Very true,'' said Samson, ''and good Sancho Panza's view of these cases is quite right.''

''Sirs, not so fast,'' said Don Quixote. ''In last year's nests there are no birds this year. I was mad—now I am in my senses; I was Don Quixote of La Mancha—I am now, as I said, Alonso Quixano the Good; and may my repentance and sincerity restore me to the esteem you used to have for me; and now let Master Notary proceed.''

''*Item*—I leave all my property absolutely to

Antonia Quixana, my niece, here present, after all has been deducted from the most available portion of it that may be required to satisfy the bequests I have made. And the first disbursement I desire to be made is the payment of the wages I owe for the time my housekeeper has served me, with twenty ducats, over and above, for a gown. The curate and the bachelor Samson Carrasco, now present, I appoint my executors.

"*Item*—It is my wish that if Antonia Quixana, my niece, desires to marry, she shall marry a man of whom it shall be first of all ascertained by information taken that he does not know what books of chivalry are; and if it should be proved that he does, and if in spite of this my niece insists upon marrying him and does marry him, then she shall forfeit the whole of what I have left her, which my executors shall devote to works of charity as they please.

"*Item*—I entreat the aforesaid gentlemen my executors, that if any happy chance should lead them to discover the author who is said to have written a history now going about under the title of 'Second Part of the Achievements of Don Quixote of La Mancha,' they beg of him on my behalf as earnestly as they can to forgive me for having been, without intending it, the cause of his writing so many and such monstrous absurdities as he has written in it; for I am leaving the world with a feeling of compunction at having provoked him to write them."

With this he closed his will, and a faintness coming over him, he stretched himself out at full length on the bed. All were in a flutter and made haste to relieve him, and during the three days he lived after that on which he made his will, he fainted away very often. The house was all in confusion; but still the niece ate and the housekeeper drank and Sancho Panza enjoyed himself; for inheriting property wipes out or softens down in the heir the feeling of grief the dead man might be expected to leave behind him.

At last Don Quixote's end came, after he had received all the sacraments, and had in full and forcible terms exprest his detestation of books of chivalry. The notary was there at the time, and he said that in no book of chivalry had he ever read of any knight-errant dying in his bed so calmly and so like a Christian as Don Quixote, who, amid the tears and lamentations of all present, yielded up his spirit—that is to say, died. On perceiving it, the curate begged the notary to bear witness that Alonso Quixano the Good, commonly called Don Quixote of La Mancha, had passed away from this present life, and died naturally; and said he desired this testimony in order to remove the possibility of any other author save Cid Hamet Benengeli bringing him to life again falsely and making interminable stories out of his achievements.

Such was the end of the Ingenious Gentleman of La Mancha, whose village Cid Hamet would not indicate precisely, in order to leave all the towns and villages of La Mancha to contend among themselves for the right to adopt him and claim him as a son, as the seven cities of Greece contended for Homer. The lamentations of Sancho and the niece and the housekeeper are omitted here, as well as the new epitaphs upon his tomb; Samson Carrasco, however, put the following:

"A doughty gentleman lies here,
A stranger all his life to fear;
Nor in his death could Death prevail,
In that last hour, to make him quail.
He for the world but little cared,
And at his feats the world was scared;
A crazy man his life he passed,
But in his senses died at last."

HANS CHRISTIAN
ANDERSEN

Born in 1805; died in 1875; went to Copenhagen to become
an actor, but, helped by friends, attended the university;
published a volume of travels in 1828, poems and a play
in 1829, and the first of his "Tales," by which his fame
abroad was established, in 1836; his "Autobiography" was
published after his death.

THE EMPEROR'S NEW CLOTHES [1]

MANY years ago there was an emperor, who
was so excessively fond of new clothes that he
spent all his money in dress. He did not trouble
himself in the least about his soldiers; nor did
he care to go either to the theater or the chase,
except for the opportunities then afforded him
for displaying his new clothes. He had a different suit for each hour of the day; and as of any
other king or emperor one is accustomed to say,
"He is sitting in council," it was always said
of him, "The Emperor is sitting in his wardrobe."

Time passed away merrily in the large town
which was his capital; strangers arrived every
day at the court. One day two rogues, calling
themselves weavers, made their appearance.
They gave out that they knew how to weave
stuffs of the most beautiful colors and elaborate
patterns, the clothes manufactured from which

---

[1] Andersen's "Tales" have attracted many translators,
among them Caroline Peachey, whose version is printed
in the Bohn Library. Another version is by Mrs. H. B.
Paull.

should have the wonderful property of remaining invisible to every one who was unfit for the office he held, or who was extraordinarily simple in character.

"These must, indeed, be splendid clothes!" thought the Emperor. "Had I such a suit, I might at once find out what men in my realm are unfit for their office, and also be able to distinguish the wise from the foolish! This stuff must be woven for me immediately." And he caused large sums of money to be given to both the weavers, in order that they might begin their work directly.

So the two pretended weavers set up two looms, and affected to work very busily, tho in reality they did nothing at all. They asked for the most delicate silk and the purest gold thread; put both into their own knapsacks; and then continued their pretended work at the empty looms until late at night.

"I should like to know how the weavers are getting on with my cloth," said the Emperor to himself, after some little time had elapsed; he was, however, rather embarrassed when he remembered that a simpleton, or one unfit for his office, would be unable to see the manufacture. "To be sure," he thought, "he had nothing to risk in his own person; but yet he would prefer sending somebody else to bring him intelligence about the weavers and their work before he troubled himself in the affair." All the people throughout the city had heard of the wonderful property the cloth was to possess; and all were anxious to learn how wise, or how ignorant, their neighbors might prove to be.

"I will send my faithful old minister to the weavers," said the Emperor at last, after some deliberation; "he will be best able to see how the cloth looks; for he is a man of sense, and no one can be more suitable for his office than he is."

So the honest old minister went into the hall, where the knaves were working with all their might at their empty looms. "What can be the meaning of this?" thought the old man, opening his eyes very wide; "I can not discover the least bit of thread on the looms!" However, he did not express his thoughts aloud.

The impostors requested him very courteously to be so good as to come nearer their looms; and then asked him whether the design pleased him, and whether the colors were not very beautiful; at same time pointing to the empty frames. The poor old minister looked and looked; he could not discover anything on the looms, for a very good reason, viz., there was nothing there. "What!" thought he again, "is it possible that I am a simpleton? I have never thought so myself; and, at any rate, if I am so, no one must know it. Can it be that I am unfit for my office? No, that must not be said either. I will never confess that I could not see the stuff."

"Well, Sir Minister!" said one of the knaves, still pretending to work, "you do not say whether the stuff pleases you."

"Oh, it is admirable!" replied the old minister, looking at the loom through his spectacles. "This pattern, and the colors—yes, I will tell the Emperor without delay how very beautiful I think them."

"We shall be much obliged to you," said the impostors, and then they named the different colors and described the patterns of the pretended stuff. The old minister listened attentively to their words, in order that he might repeat them to the Emperor; and then the knaves asked for more silk and gold, saying that it was necessary to complete what they had begun. However, they put all that was given them into their knapsacks, and continued to work with as much apparent diligence as before at their empty looms.

The Emperor now sent another officer of his court to see how the men were getting on, and to ascertain whether the cloth would soon be ready. It was just the same with this gentleman as with the minister; he surveyed the looms on all sides, but could see nothing at all but the empty frames.

"Does not the stuff appear as beautiful to you as it did to my lord the minister?" asked the impostors of the Emperor's second ambassador; at the same time making the same gestures as before, and talking of the design and colors which were not there.

"I certainly am not stupid!" thought the messenger. "It must be that I am not fit for my good, profitable office! That is very odd; however, no one shall know anything about it." And accordingly he praised the stuff he could not see, and declared that he was delighted with both colors and patterns. "Indeed, please your Imperial Majesty," said he to his sovereign, when he returned, "the cloth which the weavers are preparing is extraordinarily magnificent."

The whole city was talking of the splendid

cloth which the Emperor had ordered to be woven at his own expense.

And now the Emperor himself wished to see the costly manufacture while it was still on the loom. Accompanied by a select number of officers of the court, among whom were the two honest men who had already admired the cloth, he went to the crafty impostors, who, as soon as they were aware of the Emperor's approach, went on working more diligently than ever; altho they still did not pass a single thread through the looms.

"Is not the work absolutely magnificent?" said the two officers of the crown already mentioned. "If your Majesty will only be pleased to look at it! what a splendid design! what glorious colors!" and at the same time they pointed to the empty frames; for they imagined that every one but themselves could see this exquisite piece of workmanship.

"How is this?" said the Emperor to himself; "I can see nothing; this is, indeed, a terrible affair! Am I a simpleton? or am I unfit to be an Emperor? that would be the worst thing that could happen. Oh, the cloth is charming," said he aloud; "it has my entire approbation." And he smiled most graciously, and looked closely at the empty looms; for on no account would he say that he could not see what two of the officers of his court had praised so much. All his retinue now strained their eyes, hoping to discover something on the looms, but they could see no more than the others; nevertheless, they all exclaimed, "Oh! how beautiful!" and advised his Majesty to have some new clothes made from this splendid material for the approaching procession. "Magnificent! charming! excellent!" resounded on all sides; and every one was uncommonly gay. The Emperor shared in the general satisfaction, and presented the impostors with the ribbon of an order of knighthood to be worn in their buttonholes, and the title of "Gentlemen Weavers."

The rogues sat up the whole of the night before the day on which the procession was to take place, and had sixteen lights burning, so that every one might see how anxious they were to finish the Emperor's new suit. They pretended to roll the cloth off the looms; cut the air with their scissors; and sewed with needles without any thread in them. "See!" cried they at last, "the Emperor's new clothes are ready!"

And now the Emperor, with all the grandees of his court, came to the weavers; and the rogues raised their arms, as if in the act of holding something up, saying, "Here are your Majesty's trousers! here is the scarf! here is the mantle! The whole suit is as light as a cobweb; one might fancy one has nothing at all on, when drest in it; that, however, is the great virtue of this delicate cloth."

"Yes, indeed!" said all the courtiers, altho not one of them could see anything of this exquisite manufacture.

"If your Imperial Majesty will be graciously pleased to take off your clothes, we will fit on the new suit, in front of the looking-glass."

The Emperor was accordingly undrest, and the rogues pretended to array him in his new suit; the Emperor turning round, from side to side, before the looking-glass.

"How splendid his Majesty looks in his new clothes! and how well they fit!" every one cried out. "What a design! what colors! these are, indeed, royal robes!"

"The canopy which is to be borne over your Majesty, in the procession, is waiting," announced the chief master of the ceremonies.

"I am quite ready," answered the Emperor. "Do my new clothes fit well?" asked he, turning himself round again before the looking-glass, in order that he might appear to be examining his handsome suit.

The lords of the bed-chamber who were to carry his Majesty's train, felt about on the ground, as if they were lifting up the ends of the mantle, and pretended to be carrying something; for they would by no means betray anything like simplicity, or unfitness for their office.

So now the Emperor walked under his high canopy in the midst of the procession, through the streets of his capital; and all the people standing by, and those at the windows, cried out, "Oh! how beautiful are our Emperor's new clothes! what a magnificent train there is to the mantle! and how gracefully the scarf hangs!" in short, no one would allow that he could not see these much-admired clothes, because, in doing so, he would have declared himself either a simpleton or unfit for his office. Certainly, none of the Emperor's various suits had ever excited so much admiration as this.

"But the Emperor has nothing at all on!" said a little child. "Listen to the voice of innocence!" exclaimed his father; and what the child had said was whispered from one to another.

"But he has nothing at all on!" at last cried out all the people. The Emperor was vexed, for he knew that the people were right; but he thought "the procession must go on now!" And the lords of the bed-chamber took greater pains than ever to appear holding up a train, altho, in reality, there was no train to hold.

IVAN TURGENEFF

Born in 1818; died in 1883; educated in Moscow and St. Petersburg; studied also in Berlin; received an official appointment in 1840; began to publish poems in 1841; published a novel in 1844; his fame as an author established as early as 1850; banished to Orel, but allowed to return in 1854; lived afterward in Baden-Baden and Paris, making short visits to Russia; continued to produce novels until his death.

BAZAROV'S DEATH [1]

THE sound of a light carriage on springs—that sound which is peculiarly impressive in the wilds of the country—suddenly struck upon his hearing. Nearer and nearer rolled the light wheels; now even the neighing of the horses could be heard. Vassily Ivanovitch jumped up and ran to the little window. There drove into the courtyard of his little house a carriage with seats for two, with four horses harnessed abreast. Without stopping to consider what it could mean, with a rush of a sort of senseless joy, he ran out on to the steps. A groom in livery was opening the carriage door; a lady in a black veil and a black mantle was getting out of it.

"I am Madame Odintsov," she said. "Yevgeny Vassilyitch is still living? You are his father? I have a doctor with me."

"Benefactress!" cried Vassily Ivanovitch; and snatching her hand, he prest it convulsively to

[1] From "Fathers and Children." Translated from the Russian by Constance Garnett.

239

his lips; while the doctor brought by Anna Sergyevna, a little man in spectacles, of German physiognomy, stept very deliberately out of the carriage. "Still living, my Yevgeny is still living, and now he will be saved! Wife! wife! An angel from heaven has come to us."

"What does it mean, good Lord!" faltered the old woman, running out of the drawing-room; and comprehending nothing, she fell on the spot at Anna Sergyevna's feet, in the passage, and began kissing her garments like a madwoman.

"What are you doing!" protested Anna Sergyevna; but Arina Vlasyevna did not heed her, while Vassily Ivanovitch could only repeat, "An angel! an angel!"

"Wo ist der Kranke? [where is the patient?]" said the doctor at last, with some impatience.

Vassily Ivanovitch recovered himself. "Here, here; follow me, würdigster Herr Collega," he added through old associations.

"Ah!" articulated the German, grinning sourly.

Vassily Ivanovitch led him into the study. "The doctor from Anna Sergyevna Odintsov," he said, bending down quite to his son's ear, "and she herself is here."

Bazarov suddenly opened his eyes. "What did you say?"

"I say that Anna Sergyevna is here; and has brought this gentleman, a doctor, to you."

Bazarov moved his eyes about him. "She is here? I want to see her."

"You shall see her, Yevgeny; but first we must have a little talk with the doctor. I will tell him the whole history of your illness, since Sidor Sidoritch" (this was the name of the district

240

doctor) "has gone; and we will have a little consultation."

Bazarov glanced at the German. "Well, talk away quickly, only not in Latin: you see, I know the meaning of *jam moritur.*"

"Der Herr scheint des Deutschen mächtig zu sein," began the new follower of Æsculapius, turning to Vassily Ivanovitch.

"Ich—habe—We had better speak Russian," said the old man.

"Ah, ah! so that's how it is. To be sure—" And the consultation began.

Half an hour later, Anna Sergyevna, conducted by Vassily Ivanovitch, came into the study. The doctor had had time to whisper to her that it was hopeless even to think of the patient's recovery.

She looked at Bazarov—and stood still in the doorway; so greatly was she imprest by the inflamed and at the same time deathly face, with its dim eyes fastened upon her. She felt simply dismayed, with a sort of cold and suffocating dismay: the thought that she would not have felt like that if she had really loved him flashed instantaneously through her brain.

"Thanks," he said painfully: "I did not expect this. It's a deed of mercy. So we have seen each other again, as you promised."

"Anna Sergyevna has been so kind," began Vassily Ivanovitch.

"Father, leave us alone. Anna Sergyevna, you will allow it, I fancy, now?"

With a motion of his head he indicated his prostrate helpless frame.

Vassily Ivanovitch went out.

"Well, thanks," repeated Bazarov. "This is royally done. Monarchs, they say, visit the dying too."

"Yevgeny Vassilyitch, I hope—"

"Ah, Anna Sergyevna, let us speak the truth. It's all over with me. I'm under the wheel. So it turns out that it was useless to think of the future. Death's an old joke, but it comes fresh to every one. So far I'm not afraid—but there, senselessness is coming, and then it's all up!" he waved his hand feebly. "Well, what had I to say to you? I loved you! There was no sense in that even before, and less than ever now. Love is a form, and my own form is already breaking up. Better say how lovely you are! And now here you stand, so beautiful—" Anna Sergyevna gave an involuntary shudder. "Never mind, don't be uneasy. Sit down there. Don't come close to me: you know my illness is catching."

Anna Sergyevna swiftly crossed the room, and sat down in the armchair near the sofa on which Bazarov was lying.

"Noble-hearted!" he whispered. "Oh, how near, and how young, and fresh, and pure—in this loathsome room! Well, good-by! live long—that's the best of all—and make the most of it while there is time. You see what a hideous spectacle: the worm half-crusht, but writhing still. And you see, I thought too, I'd break down so many things: I wouldn't die—why should I!—there were problems to solve, and I was a giant! And now all the problem for the giant is how to die decently—tho that makes no difference. Never mind: I'm not going to turn tail."

Bazarov was silent, and began feeling with his hand for the glass. Anna Sergyevna gave him some drink: not taking off her glove, and drawing her breath timorously.

"You will forget me," he began again: "the dead's no companion for the living. My father will tell you what a man Russia is losing. That's nonsense, but don't contradict the old man. Whatever toy will comfort the child—you know. And be kind to mother. People like them aren't to be found in your great world if you look by daylight with a candle. I was needed by Russia. No, it's clear, I wasn't needed. And who is needed? The shoemaker's needed, the tailor's needed, the butcher—gives us meat—the butcher —wait a little, I'm getting mixt. There's a forest here—"

Bazarov put his hand to his brow.

Anna Sergyevna bent down to him. "Yevgeny Vassilyitch, I am here—"

He at once took his hand away, and raised himself.

"Good-by," he said with sudden force, and his eyes gleamed with their last light. "Good-by. Listen—you know I didn't kiss you then. Breathe on the dying lamp, and let it go out."

Anna Sergyevna put her lips to his forehead.

"Enough!" he murmured, and dropt back on to the pillow. "Now—darkness—"

Anna Sergyevna went softly out. "Well?" Vassily Ivanovitch asked her in a whisper.

"He has fallen asleep," she answered, scarce audibly. Bazarov was not fated to awaken. Toward evening he sank into complete unconsciousness, and the following day he died. Father

Alexey performed the last rites of religion over him. When they anointed him with the last unction, when the holy oil touched his breast, one eye opened; and it seemed as tho at the sight of the priest in his vestments, the smoking censers, the light before the image, something like a shudder of horror passed over the death-stricken face. When at last he had breathed his last, and there arose a universal lamentation in the house, Vassily Ivanovitch was seized by a sudden frenzy. "I said I should rebel," he shrieked hoarsely, with his face inflamed and distorted, shaking his fist in the air, as tho threatening some one; "and I rebel, I rebel!" But Arina Vlasyevna, all in tears, hung upon his neck, and both fell on their faces together. "Side by side," Anfisushka related afterward in the servants' room, "they drooped their poor heads like lambs at noonday."

But the heat of noonday passes, and evening comes and night; and then, too, the return to the kindly refuge, where sleep is sweet for the weary and heavy-laden.

HENRIK IBSEN

Born in Norway in 1828, died in 1906; studied medicine, but devoted himself to literature; his first dramatic work published in 1850; went to the University in Christiania in 1850; for a time edited a weekly paper at Christiania; became manager of a theater at Bergen in 1852; visited Germany in 1852; returned to Christiania as director of the Norwegian Theater in 1857; thereafter wrote plays continuously; lived in later years first at Dresden and then at Munich.

THE THOUGHT CHILD [1]

The action passes in the first half of the Thirteenth Century. Present: Skule; Jatgeir the Skald, an Icelander; Paul Flida, a nobleman.

JATGEIR [*enters from the back*]—Forgive my coming, lord King.

King Skule—You come to my wish, Skald!

Jatgeir—I overheard some townsfolk at my lodging talking darkly of—

King Skule—Let that wait. Tell me, Skald, you who have fared far abroad in strange lands —have you ever seen a woman love another's child? Not only be kind to it—'tis not that I mean; but *love* it, love it with the warmest passion of her soul.

Jatgeir—That can only those women do who have no child of their own to love.

King Skule—Only those women—?

Jatgeir—And chiefly women who are barren.

[1] From the translation of "The Pretenders" by William Archer.

King Skule—Chiefly the barren—? They love the children of others with all their warmest passion?

Jatgeir—That will oftentimes befall.

King Skule—And does it not sometimes befall that such a barren woman will slay another's child, because she herself has none?

Jatgeir—Ay, ay; but in that she does unwisely.

King Skule—Unwisely?

Jatgeir—Ay, for she gives the gift of sorrow to her whose child she slays.

King Skule—Think you the gift of sorrow is a great good?

Jatgeir—Yes, lord.

King Skule [*looking fixedly at him*]—Methinks there are two men in you, Icelander. When you sit amid the household at the merry feast, you draw cloak and hood over all your thoughts; when one is alone with you, sometimes you seem to be of those among whom one were fain to choose his friend. How comes it?

Jatgeir—When you go to swim in the river, my lord, you would scarce strip you where the people pass by to church: you seek a sheltered privacy.

King Skule—True, true.

Jatgeir—My soul has a like shyness; therefore I do not strip me when there are many in the hall.

King Skule—Hm. [*A short pause.*] Tell me, Jatgeir, how came you to be a skald? Who taught you skaldcraft?

Jatgeir—Skaldcraft can not be taught, my lord.

King Skule—Can not be taught? How came it then?

246

Jatgeir—I got the gift of sorrow, and I was a skald.

King Skule—Then 'tis the gift of sorrow the skald has need of?

Jatgeir—I needed sorrow; others there may be who need faith, or joy—or doubt—

King Skule—Doubt, as well?

Jatgeir—Ay; but then must the doubter be strong and sound.

King Skule—And whom call you the unsound doubter?

Jatgeir—He who doubts his own doubt.

King Skule [*slowly*]—That, methinks, were death.

Jatgeir—'Tis worse; 'tis neither day nor night.

King Skule [*quickly, as if shaking off his thoughts*]—Where are my weapons? I will fight and act, not think. What was it you would have told me when you came?

Jatgeir—'Twas what I noted in my lodgings. The townsmen whisper together secretly, and laugh mockingly, and ask if we be well assured that King Hakon is in the west land: there is somewhat they are in glee over.

King Skule—They are men of Viken, and therefore against me.

Jatgeir—They scoff because King Olaf's shrine could not be brought out to the mote-stead when we did you homage; they say it boded ill.

King Skule—When next I come to Nidaros the shrine shall out! It shall stand under the open sky, tho I should have to tear down St. Olaf's church and widen the mote-stead over the spot where it stood.

Jatgeir—That were a strong deed; but I shall

make a song of it as strong as the deed itself.

King Skule—Have you many unmade songs within you, Jatgeir?

Jatgeir—Nay, but many unborn; they are conceived one after the other, come to life, and are brought forth.

King Skule—And if I, who am king and have the might—if I were to have you slain, would all the unborn skald-thoughts within you die along with you?

Jatgeir—My lord, it is a great sin to slay a fair thought.

King Skule—I ask not if it be a *sin:* I ask if it be *possible!*

Jatgeir—I know not.

King Skule—Have you never had another skald for your friend, and has he never unfolded to you a great and noble song he thought to make?

Jatgeir—Yes, lord.

King Skule—Did you not then wish that you could slay him, to take his thought and make the song yourself?

Jatgeir—My lord, I am not barren: I have children of my own; I need not to love those of other men. [*Goes.*]

King Skule [*after a pause*]—The Icelander is in very deed a skald. He speaks God's deepest truth and knows it not. I am as a barren woman. Therefore I love Hakon's kingly thought-child, love it with the warmest passion of my soul. Oh that I could but adopt it! It would die in my hands. Which were best, that it should die in my hands or wax great in his? Should I ever have peace of soul if that came to pass? Can I forego all? Can I stand by and see Hakon make himself famous for all time? How dead and empty is all within me—and around me. No friend—ah, the Icelander! [*Goes to the door and calls.*] Has the skald gone from the palace?

A Guard [*outside*]—No, my lord: he stands in the outer hall talking with the watch.

King Skule—Bid him come hither. [*Goes forward to the table; presently Jatgeir enters.*] I can not sleep, Jatgeir: 'tis all my great kingly thoughts that keep me awake, you see.

Jatgeir—'Tis with the king's thoughts as with the skald's, I doubt not. They fly highest and grow quickest when there is night and stillness around.

King Skule—Is it so with the skald's thoughts?

Jatgeir—Ay, lord: no song is born by daylight; it may be written down in the sunshine, but it makes itself in the silent night.

King Skule—Who gave you the gift of sorrow, Jatgeir?

Jatgeir—She whom I loved.

King Skule—She died, then?

Jatgeir—No, she deceived me.

King Skule—And then you became a skald?

Jatgeir—Ay, then I became a skald?

King Skule [*seizes him by the arm*]—What gift do I need to become a king?

Jatgeir—Not the gift of doubt; else would you not question so.

King Skule—What gift do I need?

Jatgeir—My lord, you *are* a king.

King Skule—Have you at all times full faith that you are a skald?

Jatgeir [*looks silently at him for a while*]— Have you never loved?

King Skule—Yes, once—burningly, blissfully, and in sin.

Jatgeir—You have a wife.

King Skule—Her I took to bear me sons.

Jatgeir—But you have a daughter, my lord— a gracious and noble daughter.

King Skule—Were my daughter a son, I would not ask you what gift I need. [*Vehemently.*] I must have some one by me who sinks his own will utterly in mine—who believes in me, unflinchingly, who will cling close to me in good hap and ill, who lives only to shed light and warmth over my life, and must die if I fall. Give me counsel, Jatgeir Skald!

Jatgeir—Buy yourself a dog, my lord.

King Skule—Would no man suffice?

Jatgeir—You would have to search long for such a man.

King Skule [*suddenly*]—Will *you* be that man to me, Jatgeir? Will *you* be a son to me? You shall have Norway's crown to your heritage—the whole land shall be yours, if you will be a son to me, and live for my life work, and believe in me.

Jatgeir—And what should be my warranty that I did not feign—?

King Skule—Give up your calling in life, sing no more songs, and then will I believe you!

Jatgeir—No, lord: that were to buy the crown too dear.

King Skule—Bethink you well: 'tis greater to be a king than a skald.

Jatgeir—Not always.

King Skule—'Tis but your unsung songs you must sacrifice!

Jatgeir—Songs unsung are ever the fairest.

King Skule—But I must—I *must* have one who can trust in me! Only one. I feel it: had I that I were saved!

Jatgeir—Trust in yourself and you will be saved!

Paul Flida [*enters hastily*]—King Skule, look to yourself! Hakon Hakonsson lies off Elgjarness with all his fleet!

King Skule—Off Elgjarness! Then he is close at hand.

Jatgeir—Get we to arms then! If there be bloodshed to-night, I will gladly be the first to die for you!

King Skule—You, who would not live for me!

Jatgeir—A man can die for another's life work; but if he go on living, he must live for his own. [*Goes.*]

COUNT LEO TOLSTOY

Born in 1828; educated at the University of Kazan; served
in the army and commander of a battery in the Crimea in
1855, being present at the storming of Sebastopol; sent as a
special courier to St. Petersburg; lived on his estate after
the liberation of the serfs, working with the peasants and
devoting himself to literary work; published "War and
Peace" in 1865-68, "Anna Karenina" in 1875-78, "Sebastopol" in 1853-55, "Childhood, Boyhood and Youth," and "The
Kreutzer Sonata" in 1890, and "War" in 1892.

SHAKESPEARE NOT A GREAT GENIUS [1]

I REMEMBER the astonishment I felt when I
first read Shakespeare. I expected to receive
a powerful esthetic pleasure, but having read,
one after the other, works regarded as his best:
"King Lear," "Romeo and Juliet," "Hamlet"
and "Macbeth," not only did I feel no delight,
but I felt an irresistible repulsion and tedium,
and doubted as to whether I was senseless in
feeling works regarded as the summit of perfection by the whole of the civilized world to
be trivial and positively bad, or whether the
significance which this civilized world attrib-
utes to the works of Shakespeare was itself
senseless. My consternation was increased by
the fact that I always keenly felt the beauties
of poetry in every form; then why should artistic
works recognized by the whole world as those

[1] From "A Critical Essay on Shakespeare," published in
1907.

of a genius—the works of Shakespeare—not only fail to please me, but be disagreeable to me? For a long time I could not believe in myself, and during fifty years, in order to test myself, I several times recommenced reading Shakespeare in every possible form, in Russian, in English, in German and in Schlegel's translation, as I was advised. Several times I read the dramas and the comedies and historical plays, and I invariably underwent the same feelings: repulsion, weariness, and bewilderment. At the present time, being desirous once more to test myself, I have, as an old man of seventy-five, again read the whole of Shakespeare, including the historical plays, the "Henrys," "Troilus and Cressida," the "Tempest," "Cymbeline," and I have felt, with even greater force, the same feelings—this time, however, not of bewilderment, but of firm, indubitable conviction that the unquestionable glory of a great genius which Shakespeare enjoys, and which compels writers of our time to imitate him and readers and spectators to discover in him non-existent merits—thereby distorting their esthetic and ethical understanding—is a great evil, as is every untruth.

Altho I know that the majority of people so firmly believe in the greatness of Shakespeare that in reading this judgment of mine they will not admit even the possibility of its justice, and will not give it the slightest attention, nevertheless I will endeavor, as well as I can, to show why I believe that Shakespeare can not be recognized either as a great genius, or even as an average author. . . .

However hopeless it may seem, I will endeavor

to demonstrate in the selected drama—"King Lear"—all those faults equally characteristic also of all the other tragedies and comedies of Shakespeare, on account of which he not only is not representing a model of dramatic art, but does not satisfy the most elementary demands of art recognized by all.

Dramatic art, according to the laws established by those very critics who extol Shakespeare, demands that the persons represented in the play should be, in consequence of actions proper to their characters, and owing to a natural course of events, placed in positions requiring them to struggle with the surrounding world to which they find themselves in opposition, and in this struggle should display their inherent qualities.

In "King Lear" the persons represented are indeed placed externally in opposition to the outward world, and they struggle with it. But their strife does not flow from the natural course of events nor from their own characters, but is quite arbitrarily established by the author, and therefore can not produce on the reader the illusion which represents the essential condition of art.

Lear has no necessity or motive for his abdication; also, having lived all his life with his daughters, has no reason to believe the words of the two elders and not the truthful statement of the youngest; yet upon this is built the whole tragedy of his position.

Similarly unnatural is the subordinate action: the relation of Gloucester to his sons. The positions of Gloucester and Edgar flow from the circumstance that Gloucester, just like Lear, immediately believes the coarsest untruth and does not even endeavor to inquire of his injured son whether what he is accused of be true, but at once curses and banishes him. The fact that Lear's relations with his daughters are the same as those of Gloucester to his sons makes one feel yet more strongly that in both cases the relations are quite arbitrary, and do not flow from the characters nor the natural course of events. Equally unnatural, and obviously invented, is the fact that all through the tragedy Lear does not recognize his old courtier, Kent, and therefore the relations between Lear and Kent fail to excite the sympathy of the reader or spectator. The same, in a yet greater degree, holds true of the position of Edgar, who, unrecognized by any one, leads his blind father and persuades him that he has leapt off a cliff, when in reality Gloucester jumps on level ground.

These positions, into which the characters are placed quite arbitrarily, are so unnatural that the reader or spectator is unable not only to sympathize with their sufferings but even to be interested in what he reads or sees. This in the first place.

Secondly, in this, as in the other dramas of Shakespeare, all the characters live, think, speak, and act quite unconformably with the given time and place. The action of "King Lear" takes place 800 years B.C., and yet the characters are placed in conditions possible only in the Middle Ages: participating in the drama are kings, dukes, armies, and illegitimate children, and gentlemen, courtiers, doctors, farmers, officers, soldiers, and knights with vizors, etc. It is possible that such anachronisms (with which Shakespeare's dramas abound) did not injure the possibility of illusion in the sixteenth century and the beginning of the seventeenth, but in our time it is no longer possible to follow with interest the development of events which one knows could not take place in the conditions which the author describes in detail. The artificiality of the positions, not flowing from the natural course of events, or from the nature of the characters, and their want of conformity with time and space, is further increased by those coarse embellishments which are continually added by Shakespeare and intended to appear particularly touching. The extraordinary storm during which King Lear roams about the heath, or the grass which for some reason he puts on his head—like Ophelia in "Hamlet"—or Edgar's attire, or the fool's speeches, or the appearance of the helmeted horseman, Edgar—all these effects not only fail to enhance the impression, but produce an opposite effect. *"Man sieht die Absicht und man wird verstimmt,"* as Goethe says. It often happens that even during these obviously intentional efforts after effect, as, for instance, the dragging out by the legs of half a dozen corpses, with which all Shakespeare's tragedies terminate, instead of feeling fear and pity, one is tempted rather to laugh.

END OF VOLUME VIII